Consciousness Recovered

Advances in Consciousness Research

Advances in Consciousness Research provides a forum for scholars from different scientific disciplines and fields of knowledge who study consciousness in its multifaceted aspects. Thus the Series will include (but not be limited to) the various areas of cognitive science, including cognitive psychology, linguistics, brain science and philosophy. The orientation of the Series is toward developing new interdisciplinary and integrative approaches for the investigation, description and theory of consciousness, as well as the practical consequences of this research for the individual and society.

Series C: Research profiles. Presentations of significant personal and team contributions to the empirical study of consciousness.

Volume 40

Consciousness Recovered:
Psychological functions and origins of conscious thought
by George Mandler

Consciousness Recovered

Psychological functions and origins of conscious thought

George Mandler
University of California, San Diego/University College London

John Benjamins Publishing Company
Amsterdam / Philadelphia

The paper used in this publication meets the minimum requirements of the American National Standard for Information Sciences – Permanence of Paper for Printed Library Materials, ANSI Z39.48-1984.

Books by George Mandler

The language of psychology (with William Kessen)
Thinking: From association to Gestalt (with Jean Matter Mandler)
Mind and emotion
Mind and body: Psychology of emotion and stress
Cognitive psychology: An essay in cognitive science
Human nature explored
Interesting times: An encounter with the 20th century

Library of Congress Cataloging-in-Publication Data

George Mandler

Consciousness Recovered : Psychological functions and origins of conscious thought / George Mandler.

p. cm. (Advances in Consciousness Research, ISSN 1381-589X ; v. 40)

Includes bibliographical references and indexes.

1. Consciousness. I. Title. II. Series.

BF311 .M228 2002

153--dc21 2002016315

ISBN 978 90 272 5160 2 (EUR) / 978 1 58811 187 6 (US) (Pb ; alk. paper)

ISBN 978 90 272 9786 0 (Eb)

John Benjamins Publishing Co. · P.O. Box 36224 · 1020 ME Amsterdam · The Netherlands
John Benjamins North America · P.O. Box 27519 · Philadelphia PA 19118-0519 · USA

Table of contents

Preface

Just as practically everything else in human affairs the writing of this book was overdetermined and contingent on some near chance events. In 1998 Professor Maxim Stamenov suggested that I might be interested in publishing my — variously speculative — papers on consciousness in a coherent book format. I was surprised, primarily because the philosophical movers and shakers of the consciousness industry had little in common with my approach, and on my part I stayed away from trumpeted conferences or overwrought internet chat groups and news groups. But I was getting restless, getting close to finishing my recollections and some other papers left over from a busy life for attention in retirement. Some friends whose opinion I solicited as to the advantages of undertaken such an enterprise, generally replied: Only if you really want to do that. But then I found other attractive projects to be pursued, and I decided to get to the book project within two to three years.

And then one day — surfing the internet — I came upon a dated (1996?) electronic exchange about the origin of the contemporary fuss and feathers about the nature and function of consciousness. In the course of the exchange, Valerie Hardcastle said: "I think [the] honor [for the 'the first unabashed discussion of consciousness as a legitimate scientific problem since the demise of Behaviorism'] should go to George Mandler and his 1975 *Consciousness: Respectable, Useful, and Probably Necessary.* Certainly that essay is widely heralded in cognitive science as kicking off our most recent fascination with consciousness." I had known Valerie when she was a graduate student at UC San Diego and we met a couple of times to discuss my (psychological) approach to consciousness. Valerie is one of the few philosophers who take psychological (and neuroscientific) evidence seriously when discussing consciousness. Anyway, the quote came close to convincing me that I should get started on this book.

By early 2000 most of my current projects were nearing completion and the various rivulets described above combined and lapped at my computer screen. I reread the 1975 paper and found it still to a large extent serviceable. And so — I started looking at all the other papers.

But then the idea of merely rehashing old papers rapidly yielded to some theoretical notions about the origins of consciousness that had been kicking around at the edges of my own consciousness. And so the second half of Chapter 2 was born and the rest of the book became a rethinking and rewriting of some of my previous thoughts on consciousness, and with the addition of some new material in the service both of illustrating the uses of consciousness and of relating these uses to its evolution and origins I had a book in mind. So — thank you for those who made me start thinking about this project — sorry to lay partial responsibility for this child on your shoulders. Besides consciousness has by now truly become respectable, admitted by some to be useful, and by some fewer as necessary.

Introduction

Prejudices and prolegomena

I enter on this enterprise with a distinct bias — I am a psychologist, and interested in psychological explanations of human thought and action. Partly by dint of training, ideological inclination, and past career, I feel no need to speculate about the neurophysiology of consciousness. Not since the late 19th century have psychologists (or any behavioral scientists) been committed to the direct reduction of psychological to physiological phenomena. That position today is reserved for some benighted philosophers and kindred spirits who insist on bypassing psychological concepts and explanations. My own position can be illustrated by a more general view of reduction in the sciences.

I advocate a *principle of phenomenal priority (PPP)*. PPP states that, from a relatively loose view of the hierarchy of fields of knowledge, phenomena at a more complex level need to be discovered and defined before they can be explained/interpreted at a lower (usually "simpler" and more physical) level. Let me illustrate in terms of some well-know examples: (a) Exploration of the structure of DNA was not possible without the much prior "discovery" of genes by Mendel; (b) Galileo, Brahe, Kepler and Copernicus needed to discover the movement of planets before Newton could describe them in terms of a mathematical model of gravitation and attraction; (c) staying with Newton, even the apocryphal bouncing apple may have been a necessary antecedent to the law of gravitation; (d) no bacterial or viral sources of diseases are likely to be "discovered" before the disease entities are identified; (e) extensive observations of the variation of species were necessary before Wallace and Darwin could imagine a process of selection; (f) in psychology observations of the neurophysiological mechanisms underlying vision and audition were not fruitful until a reasonable level of explanation of visual and auditory phenomena at the behavioral level had been achieved.

Similar suggestions have been made before, and I do not lay sole claim to what is mostly a heuristic device, and there are also instances in which discovery and explanation of phenomena is the result of work within a particular theory or discipline, and there are closed end explanations that are simply not conducive to investigation at the "lower" level. But much of science depends on hierarchical feedforward and feedback. Concerning psychology and sociology, it should be obvious where these fields get most of their prior phenomena — from accumulated experience and the common language, much of which is colored by the society and culture whence it is obtained.

Now to apply PPP specifically to the case of psychology. In general, the understanding, reduction, and explanation of psychological phenomena in terms of neurophysiological knowledge has a long and honorable history. The result are bridging statements and an understanding how the material basis of mind, i.e., the brain, does its work. There are however occasional attempts to eliminate the psychological bridge between the common experience and the neurophysiology of the organism. Can one understand the human being fully in terms of physiology alone? Is there any reason to expect that complex (mental) phenomena can be exhaustively understood (reduced) to more basic (physiological) ones?[1]

The current preoccupation with brain imaging should be seen in the context of the PPP — the need for phenomena to be explained. In the long run imaging studies of the brain depend to a large extent on trying to find ways of mapping experiential and psychological phenomena into brain functions. With a periodicity of about 40–50 years (1900, 1950, 1990) psychology has been preoccupied with a neuropsychological view of its behavioral domain. Each time our understanding of the brain mechanisms underlying psychological phenomena improved and benefited from the intervening psychological and behavioral work. However, it seems that mere prospecting in the brain is not particular useful. To find that some psychological/behavioral function has a neural correlate is — in the absence of theory or integrative conception — not particularly impressive. What would be astounding would be a behavioral function for which no brain correlate can be found.

All of this motivates in part my almost exclusive concentration on psychological and behavioral aspects of consciousness. I am a psychologist and a materialist — I believe that all psychological phenomena have a physical basis without being reducible to it. But for the time being our psychological understanding of consciousness is incomplete — we do not yet know what it is for which we seek the physiological basis. It is not until we have a solid and preferably consensual understanding of consciousness that a neuropsychology of it will be timely, consistent, and will command general agreement. Consider trying to find the neurophysiological basis of the difference between implicit and explicit memory without having established the distinction psychologically in the first place — or any number of similar examples. At the present time, there are more varieties of neuropsychological descriptions of consciousness than there are psychological/behavioral ones. That situation is unlikely to advance their amalgamation.

I shall start with an unchanged reproduction of my 1975 paper which opened up the problem of consciousness to me, and possibly did the same to others. Apart from parenthetical comments in the body of the text to signal important changes of mind over the ensuing 25–30 years or flags to contemporary preoccupations, nothing is changed. In the end I decided that the chapter was a good presentation of what I think that consciousness does, or rather how conscious mental acts are useful and helpful. What needed some changes, which will be apparent in the rest of the book, are some of the mechanisms involved, specifically in attention and in the unnecessary notion of consciousness as an area or subsystem or domain.

In Chapter 2 I start with a brief discussion of the history of unconsciousness, but devote most of the chapter to a discussion of a possible scenario for the evolution of consciousness. My main reason is that this particular speculative approach (speculative as are all other "descriptions" of the evolution of human thought and behavior) contrasts conscious with unconscious processes and puts as one particular characteristic of conscious processes their importance, relevance, usefulness to the ongoing behavior and actions of the individual. That particular frame will be particular helpful in some of the subsequent discussions. But while helpful, the rest does not depend on these speculations; it stands equally well alone.

Chapter 3 is a discussion of how conscious contents are constructed, the role of schemas in that construction, and other issues related to the functions and structure of consciousness.

Chapter 4 then discusses briefly other approaches to consciousness. It has always been my belief that the best strategy in a scientific discussion is to present one's own view as best one can, and not to engage in lengthy discussions or cat fights with one's competitors. I will briefly discuss other psychologists and neuroscientists, but will be dyspeptic with respect to philosophers, who — I believe — have mainly muddied the waters.

Chapter 5 deals with special issues in human psychology that are affected by the nature and functions of consciousness, specifically such issues as attention, memory, and dreams.

Chapter 6 addresses the construction of emotion and pain, for two reasons. First because conscious processes are particularly important in emotional states, and second because I have spent much time and writing on issues of emotion and stress.

Chapter 7 is a brief conclusion to my presentation.

That is the plan. I will only update the issues directly addressed, and I am not concerned with an exhaustive bibliography of my coworkers in the vineyards of consciousness. The book represents my previous engagement with relevant issues, updated with new developments when these have changed the landscape. By leaving in many references that hark back several decades I hope to discourage the historical amnesia that has invaded many of the cognitive sciences.

Chapter 1

Consciousness

Respectable, useful, and probably necessary

The story started with Robert Solso when, sometime in 1973/74, he invited me to contribute to the Loyola Symposium in Chicago. It was a good time to try to think of new directions. My laboratory was going full steam with a fine group of graduate students, I had recently restarted my interests in emotion, and all work and research was going well. I had nagged at the edges of consciousness for some time and maybe it was time to sketch out a position — in the hope that it would generate both heat and light. There was some interest in such an enterprise, but little inclination to do anything about it. As I note below there were some other foolhardy psychologists willing to speculate about consciousness, and philosophers had not generally discovered their new cottage industry. When it finally saw the light of print, some unenlightened followers of the behaviorist interlude were embarrassed by the piece, but others began to argue constructively with some of its assertions. Within a few years it seemed alright to talk about consciousness again.

The chapter was rather ambitious in conception. In the absence of any similar recent piece, I felt compelled to cover much of what consciousness might touch. In fact my interest — as will be obvious in the course of the book — was always motivated by three aspect of consciousness: its seriality, limited capacity, and emphasis on important aspects of our world. So here it is, with contemporary comments in brackets, but otherwise essentially as it was published in 1975. The chapter started somewhat grandiously:

I welcome this opportunity to act as *amicus curiae* on behalf of one of the central concepts of cognitive theory — consciousness [*it was of course nothing of the sort — and still isn't*].[2] Another statement, however imperfect, may be useful to undo the harm that consciousness suffered during fifty years (approximately 1910 to 1960) in the oubliettes of behaviorism. It is additionally needed because so many of us have a history of collaboration with the keepers of the jail and to speak freely of the need for a concept of consciousness still ties the tongues of not a few cognitive psychologists.

I hope to show that consciousness is respectable in the sense that it has become the object of serious and impressive experimental research; it is useful because it avoids circumlocutions as well as constructions, such as short-term memory and focal attention, that are more easily addressed by an appeal to consciousness as part of the apparatus of cognition; and it is probably necessary because it serves to tie together many disparate but obviously related mental concepts, including attention [*and I have certainly changed my mind about that*], perceptual elaboration, and limited capacity notions.

The revival of consciousness

The history of consciousness is strewn with philosophical, theological, and pedestrian semantic debris; the history of unconscious concepts has, by inherited contrast, suffered similarly. Having made the decision to recall the concept of consciousness to service, it is useful to start baldly with the distinction between conscious and unconscious processes. I do so with some sense of embarrassment vis-a-vis the contributions of others. Freud, in particular, has contributed much to the finer distinctions among shadings of the unconscious. However, if we are to make a fresh start within the experimental investigation of consciousness, we shall probably also have to rediscover these distinctions within the new realm of discourse. For present purposes the distinctions among preconscious, preattentive, primary processes, and unconscious are premature [*but I soon introduced similar distinctions*]. It suffices to distinguish those processes that are accessible to consciousness and those that are not. We shall note that Neisser, for example, assumes that the product of preattentive (preconscious) processes are holistic, vague, and unelaborated. It is not at all certain that current research on reading and language production and comprehension will bear out this assumption. Miller,[3] following Freud, set a distinct boundary between preconscious and unconscious processes, implying that the latter are inaccessible. The evidence suggests that accessibility of unconscious processes shades from the readily accessible to the inaccessible. In what follows I shall have repeated occasions to use the various different terms of consciousness as they occur in context. However, the intent, from my vantage point, is — at this time — to distinguish only between the contents of consciousness and unconscious processes. The latter include those that are not available to conscious experience, be they feature analyzers, deep syntactic structures, affective appraisals, computational processes, language production systems, action system of many kinds, or whatever.

Much of what we know and say today about consciousness has been known and said by others before us, in the past hundred years by Wundt, the Würzburgers, Lashley, and many others. I only want to summarize here the high points of a modern view of consciousness as it has developed, or rather revived, during the development of a disciplined and highly structured new view of cognitive psychology. The development of this viewpoint was tentative, as one would expect it to be against the background of the established dogma of behaviorism in the United States. In 1962, George A. Miller, one of the prophets of the new mentalism of the 1970s, started off his discussion of consciousness by suggesting that we "ban the word [consciousness] for a decade or two until we can develop more precise terms for the several uses which 'consciousness' now obscures (p. 25)." More than a decade has passed and we seem to be doing as prescribed without any intervening banishment. Most current thought on the topic was, as a matter of fact, well summarized by Miller. Following William James, Miller stressed the selective functions of consciousness — the notion that only some part of all the possible experiences that are available at any point in time and space is selected for conscious expression. [*Eventually I thought that the criteria for such selection are important in the function of consciousness*] Miller also noted what we will stress again later, [*but reject today*] namely that "the selective function of consciousness and the limited span of attention are complementary ways of talking about the same thing (p. 49)." And, with Lashley, he reminds us that "[it] is the result of thinking, not the process of thinking that appears spontaneously in consciousness (p. 56)." It is well to keep that last statement in mind, because it is an important part of the new mentalism, of modern cognitive psychology, of the human information processing approach. "Thinking" or cognition or information processing for the psychologist is a term that refers to theoretical processes, complex transformations on internal and external objects, events, and relations. These processes are not conscious; they are, in the first instance, constructions generated by the psychological theorist. By definition the conscious individual cannot be conscious — in any acceptable sense of the term — of theoretical processes invoked to explain his actions. In the same sense, the term mind refers to the totality of theoretical processes that are ascribed to the individual. To accept this point of view avoids the solipsisms and sophisms of philosophies of mind. [*Of all the things that had been said before the current deluge, I wish philosophers had heard this. It would have avoided their continuous confusion between mind and consciousness*] The important advances in our excursions into consciousness must come through the usual interplay of empirical investigation and imaginative theory. The functions of consciousness are slowly being investigated and the beginnings of theoretical integrations of the concept of consciousness into cognitive models are emerging.

As a prolegomenon to theory and better understanding of private knowledge, Natsoulas[4] has examined the content of "introspective awareness." Although he does not present us with any conclusions, Natsoulas has provided a partial list of the problems that psychologists and philosophers encounter when they want to deal directly with these contents. We have, in general, not gone far beyond a listing, since it is obviously too early to argue for a specific model of private experience or consciousness — it does not exist, not even in the broadest outline. However, some of the necessary first steps have been taken to build some of the components that such a theory must accommodate. At the same time, psychologists are becoming sensitive to the need for a critical evaluation of common sense and philosophical notions about consciousness. Many phenomenologically oriented philosophers and psychologists are still wedded to a Wundtian idea that psychology should be the study of conscious mental events, whereas unconscious (mental) mechanisms are to be left to some other world such as physiology.

In modern theory, one of the most influential books, Neisser's *Cognitive psychology*,[5] was strangely circumspect about the problem of consciousness. Was it too early then to talk openly about Imperial Psychology's clothes? Not that Neisser avoids the subject — he clearly talks about consciousness though one comes upon it in circuitous ways. In his final chapter Neisser tackles the relationship between iconic memory and consciousness; he comes to consciousness via the attentive processes in visual perception and thence to memory. He notes that the constructive processes in memory "themselves never appear in consciousness, their products do" (p. 301). And in rational problem solving the executive processes "share many of the properties of focal attention in vision and of analysis-by-synthesis in hearing (p. 302)." Noting the distinction between primary and secondary processes,[6] he asserts that rational and therefore presumably conscious thought operates as a secondary process — elaborating often unconscious, probably unlearned primary process operations in the Freudian sense. The products of the primary process alone, preceding consciousness and attention, are only "fleetingly" conscious unless elaborated by secondary processes. By implication the elaboration by secondary processes is what produces fully conscious events. By tentative implication primary processes are "like" preattentive processes in vision and hearing, the conscious processes are "like" focal attention. The secondary processes elaborate and select. We shall hear similar arguments from Posner and Shallice shortly. However, Neisser's contribution to the study of consciousness is in his discussion of preattentive processes and focal attention. When we turn to these processes, the clues from Neisser's final chapter open up a major contribution to the theory of consciousness. I apologize for the Talmudic exegesis before coming to this point, but it does, I believe, illustrate the gingerly and skitterish way in which psychologists, up until very recently, have permitted themselves to talk about consciousness.[7]

In Chapter 4, Neisser starts by taking the term "focal attention" straight from Schachtel,[8] a psychoanalyst whose history has not prevented a frank discussion of these forbidden topics. If you will, in what follows, permit the free translation of "attention" into consciousness, you will note why Neisser's contribution is important. First, "attention … is an allotment of analysing mechanisms to a limited region of the field (p. 88)." In other words, consciousness is a limited capacity mechanism. On the other hand, preattentive processes, that is, processes that are not in attention but precede it, have the function of forming the objects of attention. [*Today I would probably say that these preattentive processes should be assigned to the notion of attention, whereas attention, as Neisser uses it, is more like what we call consciousness*] Some of these preattentive processes (the primary processes of the final chapter) are innate. Many actions are under such preattentive control. Walking, driving and many others are "made without the use of focal attention (p. 92)." There are processes that run off outside of consciousness (unconsciously) while others do not. "More permanent storage of information requires an act of attention (p. 93)." Transfer to permanent storage requires consciousness. As apparently do some decisional processes. Harking back to another era, "the processes of attentive synthesis often lead to an internal verbalization (p. 103)." We often talk about the contents of consciousness.

In brief summary, then, Neisser's interpretation is in concord with much modern speculation about the role of consciousness. It is a limited-capacity mechanism, often synonymous with the notion of attention.[*I will argue later that attention involves spatio-temporal processing, whereas consciousness is concerned with mental contents*] The processes that make up consciousness are secondary processes, secondary in elaboration and time to primary, preattentive processes that are unconscious, sometimes innate and often the result of automatization. Consciousness is an area [*a locution which I now consider to be a serious mistake*] that permits decision processes of some types to operate, where the outputs from different systems may be integrated, and where transfers to long term storage systems take place. [*It is a curious comment on the history of our field that despite Ulric Neisser's important role in the development of the field his notions about consciousness and focal attention have received little, if any, development or utilization by others*]

Among the important attempts specifically to incorporate awareness notions into contemporary cognitive theory, Shallice[9] has argued for the necessity of studying phenomena of consciousness if for no other reasons than that there exist a number of concepts in current psychological theory that require the implicit or explicit postulation of some conscious mechanisms. Among these are the postulation of conscious rehearsal in primary memory and the frequent equation of attention and consciousness;[10] others are methodological, as in experiments which require subjects to monitor private experiences.[11] In his theoretical development Shallice argues for an isomorphism between phenomenal experience and information-processing concepts. Specifically he develops in some detail the notion that the content of consciousness can be identified with a selector input that determines first what particular action system will become dominant, and, second, sets the goal for the action system. [*Whereas the general approach has not been extensively pursued, even by Shallice, the selection of a "dominant" action has become an important characteristic ascribed to consciousness*]

Another approach, derived from problems of attention, has been mounted by Posner and his associates. They have focused on those mental operations which are characterized by interference effects or in other words, by a limited capacity mechanism which may be related to the "subjective experience of the unity of consciousness".[12] By studying the processes that interfere one with another and showing how limited capacity is assigned to different functions, one can "connect the operations of this limited capacity mechanism to intention, awareness, storage and other traditional functions of consciousness".[13]

Both Shallice and Posner deny any attempt to specify a mechanism of consciousness or private experience that is coextensive with common language uses of the concept. The attempt is, so to speak, from the bottom up, trying to specify with some rigor some of the mechanisms that may be isomorphic with consciousness and learn more about their operation within theoretical systems.

Posner and Boies[14] in their study of the components of attention have noted that "attention in the sense of central processing capacity is related to mental operations of which we are conscious, such as rehearsing or choosing a response … (p. 407)." Conversely, they noted that the contact between input and long-term memory is not part of this attentional (conscious) process, and in fact, the conscious component of the processing mechanism occurs, as a result, rather late in the sequence of "attentional" events [*which corresponds with my later distinction between spatio-temporal attention followed, but not always, by conscious contents*].

Posner and Klein[15] have summarized this interpretation of the use of "consciousness" within the context of experimental investigations. They suggest that it refers to operations such as rehearsal or priming that require access to a limited capacity system. Although the conscious processes are usually late in the processing sequence and follow "habitual" or preattentive encoding, they are flexible and may occur early under time pressure. Also, in a bridge to other similar views these processes are seen as setting up required responses "without depending upon the actual release of the motor program" (p. 34).

The recurrent theme of readiness for and choices among actions has also been invoked by Festinger et al.[16] They have suggested that, in part, the conscious aspect of some perceptual phenomena depends on preprogrammed sets of efferent (action) programs that a particular input puts into a state of readiness for immediate use.

The limited evidence from the experimental studies as well as from informed theory points to extensive preconscious processing which is, under some circumstances, followed by conscious processing. Much of behavior, however, is automatic and does not require conscious attention. Typically such actions are called habitual, automatic, or preprogrammed. Typically also they tend to be ballistic in form and run off with little variation.

It is far beyond the scope of this paper to discuss the problem of automaticity and the kinds of structures that occur automatically in contrast with those that require attentional, conscious work. In reference to response sequences — or action systems as I prefer to call them now — I have discussed the notion that cognitive structures or symbolic analogues of discrete actions systems develop during overlearning.[17] It is well known in the integration that occurs during skill learning, for example, driving. I allude to the problem here simply to note that much of "learned" behavior and actions can be integrated into new central structures, which then become functional units represented cognitively as single chunks and manipulable consciously in the constructions of new plans and new actions. At the action side of consciousness relatively little work has been done to describe how the limited capacity system is used in integrating representation of overt actions into larger units. Just as consciousness deals with chunks of incoming information, so must it deal with chunks of efferent actions.

In the arena of perceptual events the topic of automatic processing or encoding confronts us repeatedly as the converse of conscious processing. Posner and Warren[18] have discussed the variety of such automatic processes involved in coding mechanisms. Generally what is automatic is very much like what Neisser calls preattentive, parallel processes. In contrast, Posner and Warren note that conscious processes are more variable and that conscious constructions provide the new mnemonic devices needed to store material in long term representations. It is here that we face the insistence that new encodings for long term storage depend on a functioning conscious system.

LaBerge[19] has addressed the issue of automatization in a novel way — asking not only about the relation between automatization and attention, but also about the process whereby certain coding systems become automatized. He concludes that during postcriteria performance there occurs a gradual withdrawal of attention from the particular components of a task. Under this process of decreasing attention (consciousness?) the part of the processing involved in coding the particular perceptual material is being made automatic. Eventually much of the perceptual processing can "be carried out automatically, that is prior to the focussing of attention on the processing." LaBerge also implies that this postcriterial, overlearning process produces the integration of new, higher order units or chunks. He is obviously addressing the development of preattentive processes, and also the functional unity and autonomy of these units, particularly when he notes that often "one cannot prevent the processing once it starts." There is a useful similarity between these propositions about the development of automatic encodings and my previous discussion on the representation of overlearned action patterns.

We have here a possible distinction between two kinds of unconscious (preattentive, primary) processes. Those that are innate or preprogrammed or dependent primarily on some structural characteristics of the organism; and those that, though initially conscious, become, by some process such as overlearning, automatic and unconscious. Although the latter are easily brought into consciousness it is also intuitively likely that this might be difficult, if not impossible, for the former [*Most of these arguments still hold and I will not repeat them later*].

It seems to be agreed that consciousness is a clearing house that enters into the flow of processing under certain specifiable, but at present still not specified, conditions. Certain processes operate on conscious information generated by nonconscious (preattentive) processes. However, it bears repeating that there are important nonconscious postattentive processes that are operative subsequent to information generated by conscious processes. Many of these involve actions (which my older colleagues in psychology have inadequately called "behavior") that operate often without conscious attention. These actions and their representation systems are as complex and as finely structured as the preattentive perceptual systems. Unfortunately, partly by accidents of history, cognitive psychologists tend to be somewhat careless about specifying how organisms come to act. However, the hierarchic, structural view of action has an honorable and creative history. I would draw your attention to the most recent and important exposition of this view proposed by Gallistel.[20]

In summary, current thought has concentrated on the consciousness of the perceptual or encoding side of information flow. Some attention has been given to its functions in memory storage and retrieval. Much is still to be done at the output side. Current notions have focussed on the functions of consciousness as selecting encoded sensory information and preparing choices among appropriate action or response alternatives. Many other functions of consciousness still await detailed analyses or may be incorrect assignments to this particular system.

Conscious contents and processes

My own interest in consciousness arose in part out of a long-term project on the relation between mind and emotion, and more immediately out of some recent considerations of the limits of attention and consciousness.[21] In that presentation I argued for a direct translation between focal attention and consciousness [*One more word on that possible confusion. Since many writers at the time avoided the term "consciousness," they did often refer to what today is called consciousness as attention*]. I suggested that some of the so-called short-term memory phenomena are best assigned to the limited capacity mechanism of consciousness and that the limitations of that single conscious system in terms of dimensional analyses may serve as a bridging concept for George A. Miller's puzzle about the similar limitations he noted for both short term memory and absolute judgment.[22]

The limited capacity of "short-term" memory, the immediate memory span, as well as the limitation in absolute judgment tasks to some seven values or categories, can usefully be assigned to the limited capacity of conscious content. The limitation refers to the limited number of values on any single dimension (be it physical, acoustic. semantic or whatever) that can be kept within the conscious field.

The main points of the argument relevant to the present topic concern certain distinctions among the concepts of attention, consciousness and short-term memory. In the first instance, I want to restrict the concept of consciousness to events and operations within a limited capacity system, with the limitation referring to number of functional units or chunks that can be kept in consciousness at any one point in time. This concept has much in common with what has been called focal attention. Attentional processes are those mechanisms that deal with the selection of objects or events that occur in consciousness. Second, I want to assert a distinction between short-term memory and consciousness. The limited reach of consciousness has a respectable history, going back at least 200 years. However, it is not a memory system — it does not involve any retrieval. What is in the momentary field of consciousness is not remembered, it is psychologically present.

None of the foregoing denies the utility of the conception of different memory systems, whether long term, working, or operational. It is probably most reasonable to consider these different "systems" on a continuum of depth of processing, as proposed by Craik and Lockhart.[23] Different types of analyses require different processing depths and different processing times. But the information that, so to speak, can be "read off" the contents of consciousness is not memorial as such. Depth of processing determines how and what can be remembered. If processing time is short, or encoding "superficial," and if the code decays rapidly, it will be short; if processing is extended or if encoding is "complex," information adequate for long term retrieval or reconstruction will be stored. Within certain limits, the storage processes — at whatever depths — can only take place on conscious material; conversely, retrieval usually implies retrieval into the conscious field. However, the memory mechanisms and the contents of consciousness are two very distinct kinds of mental events.

Posner, who has contributed much to recent investigations of the structure of the limited capacity system of conscious events, suggested as early as 1967 that "operational" and "short-term" memories should be considered as different systems. The operating systems may vary à la Craik and Lockhart in their time course and their products, but they should not be confounded with the immediately given content of consciousness. The confounding of these two systems in early investigations and theories is understandable, given the very brief time course of some memory processes and the rapid changes in the focus of consciousness (attention). However, within consciousness many different kinds of operations may be performed — consciousness is not limited in the complexity of the information it draws on, only in the amount. Consciousness is modality independent, and, depending on the task facing the individual, may involve very complex and abstract operations. In general then, I will prefer to use the term consciousness to focal attention (although they may have to be interchanged) but I will differentiate strictly between consciousness and short-term memory processes, which deal with storage and retrieval.[24]

I do not intend to invoke a separate processing stage or system to accommodate the concept of consciousness. Consciousness, in the first instance, refers to a state of a structure. Certain operations and processes act on these structures which constitute conscious content. Cognitive structures, or schemas, may, under certain circumstances, become conscious, that is, enter the conscious state; when they do not, they are by definition unconscious [*This is very close to where I ended up — there is no abstract consciousness, rather some mental contents are conscious*]. Limited capacity refers to the number of such unitary structures that may be conscious at any one point in time. There is no separate system, however, that contains the conscious contents. Rather conscious structures differ from others in that certain operations, such as storage, retrieval, and choice (see below), may be performed on them.

It is beyond the intent of this chapter to discuss the origins of consciousness. It is a characteristic of the organism that certain structures can become conscious, but it is a function of human interactions with the environment that determines which structures do in fact become conscious. Piaget[25] has discussed extensively these interactions and stressed the transactions among perceptions of the self, the environment, and the development of consciousness. The development of consciousness is not, from my view, some magical burgeoning of internal awareness but rather dependent on specific organism-environment interactions. These involve, to a large part, the internalization of actions.[26] More important, however, the conditions of personal and social development determine what can and what cannot be represented in consciousness. Depending on these conditions, different individuals, groups, and cultures will have different conscious contents — different social and cultural consciousness, different realities. [*That position is consistent with my current assertions, but I have not extensively extended or developed the importance of social/cultural determinants*]. However, the primary purpose of the present chapter is to discuss how these conscious contents operate, not what they are or how they might be established.

Finally, conscious contents can be spoken about. I shall discuss later the lack of any one-to-one correspondence between consciousness and language, but this should not obscure the important relationship between private conscious events and language. It is by the use of the latter that we primarily communicate our own private view of reality, and it is in turn by the use of language that, in the adult at least, many conscious structures are manipulated and changed.

With these primarily definitional problems out of the way, I want to address first some of the ancient and admittedly complex and very special problems that the concept of consciousness poses for any psychological theory. I shall not propose any radical solutions but rather that the problem of the private datum can be approached reasonably and analytically, rather than frantically or mystically. Next, I want to sketch some of the possible uses of consciousness in cognitive theory, followed by some suggestions for the adaptive functions of consciousness. Finally, in the last section, I want to address the broader problem of the flow of consciousness and its relation to limited capacity, with particular attention to special states of consciousness.

Consciousness: A special problem for mental theory

The individual experiences feelings, attitudes, thoughts, images, ideas, beliefs and other contents of consciousness, but these contents are not accessible to anyone else. Briefly stated, that is the special problem facing psychologists. There are no evasions possible. It is not possible to build a phenomenal psychology that is shared. A theory of phenomena may be shared but the private consciousness, once expressed in words, gestures, or in any way externalized is necessarily a transformation of the private experience. No theory external to the individual, that is, one that treats the organism as the object of observation, description, and explanation, can at the same time be a theory that uses private experiences, feelings, and attitudes as data.[27] Events and objects in consciousness can never be available to the observer without having been restructured, reinterpreted, and appropriately modified by structures that are specific to the individual doing the reporting. These structures may even be specific to the kinds of experiences, feelings, and attitudes that are reported.

The content of consciousness, as philosophers and psychologists have told us for centuries, is not directly available as a datum in psychology. How then are we to deal with the contents of consciousness? Can the perennial problem of private datum and public inference at least be stated concisely in order to indicate the magnitude of the problem and possible directions for future development?

We are faced with a phenomenon that might be called the uncertainty principle of psychology. Adrian for example, noted: "The particular difficulty that the questioner may influence the answer recalls the uncertainty principle in physics, which limits the knowledge we can gain about any individual particle."[28] There are two related problems in the study of consciousness. The first is more fundamental than the question that Adrian addresses. It is not only the case that the nature of the interrogation may affect the reported content of consciousness, but, more basically, the act of examination itself may affect the individually observable conscious contents. This conjecture is reasonable even at the level of processing capacity, since the conscious act of interrogating one's conscious content must occupy some part of the limited capacity. As a result the available content is altered by the process of interrogation.

Given that the act of interrogation changes the content of consciousness, the source of that inquiry becomes of secondary importance. The second problem to be faced is the fact that the contents of consciousness are not simply reproducible by some one-to-one mapping into verbal report. Even if these contents were always couched in language, which they surely are not, some theory of transmission would be required. As a result we are faced with the individual's observation of the contents of his consciousness on the one hand, and on the other with the psychologist's theoretical inference about those contents, based on whatever data, including introspective reports, are available. Both of these knowledges may be used as relevant to the construction of a psychology of cognition, though it may in principle be impossible to determine, in any exact sense, the relation between these two interpretations of consciousness.

Private experiences are important aspects of the fully functioning mental system. It is possible to get transformed reports about those events and it should be possible to develop appropriate theories that relate contents of consciousness, their transformations, and their report. However, it is not possible to build a theory that makes direct predictions about private experience since the outcome of those predictions cannot be inspected by the psychologist/observer. This position does admit the development of private theories, by the individual about himself. To the individual his [*thirty years ago we were insensitive to gender in our speech — I let these "lapses" stand to convey the flavor of the times*] experience is a datum, and as a consequence his theories about his own structures are, within limits, testable by direct experience. These individual, personal theories of the self are both pervasive and significant in explaining human action, but they cannot, without peril, be generalized to others or to the race as a whole.[29] We note, therefore, that people's reports about their experiences, their behavior and their actions are very frequently, and may always be, fictions or theories about those events. However, it is only those reports that are available to us. Even the introspecting individual who says that his experience conforms to certain predicted aspects is making statements about derived correspondences resulting from mental transformations. Indirect scientific predictions about experiences are possible, but the test of those predictions is one step removed from the actual experiences, as are all predictions about the values of theoretical entities. If the behaviorist revolution, with all the negative influences it has had on the development of a fully theoretical psychology, has had one positive effect, it is this realization that even the complete acceptance of the importance of private experience does not thereby make it a possible end point for a scientific theory.

Some uses of consciousness

One of the important processes in which consciousness intervenes is in the testing of potential action choices and the appraisal of the situational givens. [*While this has some truth to it, I think it overstates the process*]. The relation between choice and consciousness, as we have seen, has motivated much of the recent research. The analysis of situations and appraisal of the environment, on the other hand, goes on mainly at the nonconscious level, which will be discussed in greater detail later. In any case, the outcomes of these analyses may be available in consciousness and the effect of potential actions on the present situation can be estimated and evaluated. Consciousness is a field in which potential choices are given the opportunity to be evaluated against potential outcomes. This delay produces reflective consideration and may in fact be responsible for greater "freedom" of action.[30]

Much of what is often considered to be the meaning of the common sense term "thinking" is what takes place in consciousness when the outcome of different structures, and even in some cases their composition, are evaluated and decisions are made. [*Consciousness makes it possible to do evaluations and decisions but much of the work is still done unconsciously*]. It is possible for the cognitive system to call for the testing of specific outcomes while temporarily blocking output from the system as a whole, to compare the consequences of different outcomes and to choose outcomes which produce one or another desired alternative. The notion of choice would be entirely within the context of modern choice theories,[31] and the choice itself, of course, would go through some "unconscious" cognitive structures before a "decision" is made. However, consciousness permits the comparison and inspection of various outcomes so that the choice systems which may in fact be "unconscious" can operate on these alternatives. [*Which is the better way of phrasing it*]

It appears that one of the functions of the consciousness mechanism is to bring two or more (previously unconscious) mental contents into direct juxtaposition. The phenomenal experience of choice, as a matter of fact, seems to demand exactly such an occurrence. We usually do not refer to a choice unless there is a "conscious" choice between two or more alternatives. The attribute of "choosing" is applied to a decision process between two items on a menu, several possible television programs, or two or more careers, but not to the decision process that decides whether to start walking across a street with the right or left foot, whether to scratch one's ear with a finger or the ball of the hand, or whether to take one or two sips from a cup of hot coffee. I would argue that the former cases involve the necessity of deciding between two or more choices presented to a choice mechanism at the same time, whereas the latter involve only the situationally predominant actions. However, these cases may be transferred to the conscious choice state if and when certain conditions of possible consequences and immediate adaptability supervene. Given a hot cup of coffee so labelled, I may "choose" to take one very small sip, or I may "choose" to start with my right foot in a 100-meter race, given certain information on its advantage to my time in the distance. In other words, consequences and social relevance determine which choices are conscious. More important, however, the mechanisms of choice (including the various theories of choice behavior) are not conscious. It is presumably the operation of these mechanisms on material in the conscious state that give the epiphenomenal experience of free choice, the appearance that someone (the agent) is doing the choosing. He or she is, but by the operation of unconscious mechanisms, which therefore give the appearance of voluntary choice among the conscious alternatives. Mental mechanisms "choose" among both conscious and unconscious events.

It might be noted that the so-called mentalism that philosophers talk about often refers to these "thought" processes, the outcome of unconscious mental processes that are evaluated in the "conscious" system. However, to mistake conscious mental events for much more complex nonconscious structures is surely in error and leads to the kind of naive mentalism shown in the works of some philosophers of the mind.

Evaluative activities often act on conscious content, but evaluative activities also may take place at an "unconscious" level. Clearly many cognitive structures that lead to certain outcomes and the anticipation of these outcomes (a scanning ahead of a particular structure) may switch the system from one structure to another. However, these changes are not available to inspection, and are only available to indirect inspection by the process of hypothesizing their constitution and testing these hypotheses.

If the only difference between these two kinds of evaluative actions and choices is that some take place in consciousness [*today I would say "consciously", rather than "in consciousness" — consciousness is not a place or domain*] and others do not, the end result would be a rather puny achievement for so imposing a mechanism as consciousness. I would propose initially two arguments for the distinction between conscious and unconscious evaluations and choices. First, many relational processes operate primarily, if not exclusively, on conscious content. I have already indicated this particular argument in the case of simple choice. However, there are other relational operators that seem to do their work primarily on conscious content. In addition to choice, these include evaluation, comparison, grouping, categorization, and serial ordering. In short, practically all novel relational orderings require that the events to be ordered must be simultaneously present in the conscious field. This applies to choice, as well as to relational concepts stored in memory, for example. Needless to say, there are many relational judgments that do not require conscious comparisons. To say that "a dog is an animal" makes uses of established structures and does not require a new relational operation. However, to say that "Rex looks like a cross between a dachshund and a spaniel" would presumably require conscious juxtaposition. Once relations (be they superordinate, subordinate, opposites, or whatever) have been established and stored, subsequent evaluations are frequently unconscious.

The second argument for the importance of consciousness suggests that choice and other processes that operate on conscious content are dependent on those structures that can enter the conscious state. Only those structures that can become conscious can be subjected to choice activities. Thus, situational and social relevance determine the content of consciousness and the "ideational" operations that can be performed on the individual's reality.

The possible adaptive functions of consciousness

One may look at some of these uses also from the point of view of their adaptive significance. Probably because of the unpleasantness of the past 50 or 60 years relatively little has been said about the adaptive functions of consciousness. Miller has described them in general terms and Gray has called for a more intensive look at the evolutionary significance of conscious systems.[32] In general, however, American psychologists particularly have shied away from looking at the functional significance of consciousness. This is at least surprising, since we are faced with a characteristic of the human species that is without exception. Given the rather weak evidence that psychologists have accepted as indicants for the evolutionary significance of such vague concepts as aggression and intelligence, why avoid a phenomenon as indisputably characteristic of the species as consciousness? Partly, the answer lies in the behaviorist dogma that consciousness is epiphenomenal and, by implication, has no adaptive significance. It is in part in opposition to that dogma that I want to suggest some possible directions in which speculations and investigations about the adaptiveness of consciousness might go.

There is a variety of functions that the consciousness system may perform, all of which may be said to have evolutionary significance and all of which have varying degrees of evidence for their utility and theoretical significance: [*I leave the following uncommented, but will return to some of these points in a discussion of the evolution of conscious processes*]

1. The first, and most widely addressed function of consciousness considers it as a scratch pad for the choice and selection of actions systems. Decisions are made often on the basis of possible outcomes, desirable outcomes, and appropriateness of various actions to environmental demands. Such a description comes close to what is often called "covert trial and error" behavior in the neobehaviorist literature. This function permits the organism more complex considerations of action-outcome contingencies than does the simple feedback concept of reinforcement, which alters the probability of one or another set of actions. It also permits the consideration of possible actions that the organisms has never before performed, thus eliminating the overt testing of possible harmful alternatives. In this sense the process is similar to the TOTE system of Miller, Galanter, and Pribram.[33]

2. Within the same general framework as the first function, consciousness is used to modify and interrogate long-range plans, rather than immediate-action

alternatives. In the hierarchy of actions and plans in which the organism engages, this slightly different function makes it possible to organize disparate action systems in the service of a higher plan. For example, in planning a drive to some new destination one might consider subsets of the route, or, in devising a new recipe, the creative chef considers the interactions of several known culinary achievements. Within the same realm, consciousness is used to retrieve and consider modifications in long-range planning activities. These, in turn, might be modified in light of other evidence, either from the immediate environment or from long term storage.

3. In considering actions and plans consciousness participates in retrieval programs from long-term memory, even though these retrieval programs and strategies themselves are usually not conscious. Thus, frequently, though not always, the retrieval of information from long-term storage is initiated by relatively simple commands — in program language, rather than machine language. These may be simple instructions such as, "What is his name?" or, "Where did I read about that?" or more complex instructions, such as, "What is the relation between this situation and previous ones I have encountered?" This process has the adaptive function of permitting simple addresses to complex structures.

4. Comments on the organism's current activities occur in consciousness and use available cognitive structures to construct some storable representation of current activity. Many investigators have suggested that these new codings and representations always take place in consciousness. Such processes as mnemonic devices and storage strategies apparently require the intervention of conscious structures. Certainly many of them, such as categorization and mental images, do. Once this new organization of information is stored, it may be retrieved for a variety of important purposes.

First, in the social process consciousness provides access to the memory bank which, together with an adequate system of communication, such as human language, has tremendous benefit to cooperative social efforts. Other members of the species may receive solutions to problems, thus saving time if nothing else; they may be apprised of unsuccessful alternatives, or, more generally, participate in the cultural inheritance of the group. This process requires selection and comparison among alternatives retrieved from long-term storage, all of which apparently takes place in consciousness.

Second, both general information, as well as specific sensory inputs, may be stored in either propositional or analogue form. The re-representation at some future time makes possible decision processes that depend on comparisons between current and past events, and the retrieval of relevant or irrelevant information for current problem solving.

5. Another aspect that consciousness apparently permits is a "troubleshooting" function for structures normally not represented in consciousness. There are many systems that cannot be brought into consciousness, and probably most systems that analyze the environment in the first place have that characteristic. In most of these cases only the product of cognitive and mental activities are available to consciousness; among these are sensory analyzers, innate action patterns, language-production systems, and many more. In contrast, many systems are generated and built with the cooperation of conscious processes, but later become nonconscious or automatic. These latter systems may apparently be brought into consciousness, particularly when they are defective in their particular function.[34] We all have had experiences of automatically driving a car, typing a letter, or even handling cocktail party conversation, and being suddenly brought up short by some failure such as a defective brake, a stuck key or a "You aren't listening to me." At that time, the particular representations of actions and memories involved are brought into play in consciousness, and repair work gets under way. Thus, structures that are not species specific and general but are the result of experience can be inspected and reorganized more or less easily.

Many of these functions permit the organism to react reflectively rather than automatically, a distinction that has frequently been made between humans and lower animals. All of them permit more adaptive transactions between the organism and its environment. Also, in general, the functions of consciousness permit a focusing upon the most important and species relevant aspects of the environment. The notion that attentional mechanisms select personally relevant materials and events is commonplace in attentional research [*this point became centrally important*]. The processes that define such relevance are generally unknown, although we can assume that an adaptive function of selection into consciousness exists. However, there remains the unexplored mystery of the processes of information reduction that select some aspect of the surround.

The need for a rapid reduction of all the sensory information available to an organism at any given point in time and space is obvious. If we were conscious of all the information available at the sensory surface, we would never escape from the confusion generated by our environment. [*eventually this issue became central in my evolutionary speculations*]

Consciousness (or attention) is highly selective. The sensory systems themselves are, of course, selective in the first instance. The evolutionary process has generated organisms that register only a limited amount of the information available in their environment. How these limitations from the environment to the sensory surface have developed has been the subject of some biological speculations. The reduction from the sensory surface to consciousness is even more spectacular, but we have few clues for the evolutionary reason of this reduction. We know that it exists,[35] and attention theorists have been concerned primarily with the filtering mechanisms that reduce the sensory information to the few chunks of information that reach consciousness. However, why that number should be 5 or 6 or 7, rather than 3 or 12 is still shrouded in mystery.

The limitation of conscious capacity and the flow of consciousness

One of the most perplexing results of experimental studies of consciousness has been the counterintuitive notion that consciousness seems to be discrete, relatively short, and quite transient. How does this contrast with consciousness in the common discourse? It seems to be continuous, flowing, extending without break throughout our waking hours, and just as flowing and continuous in our dreams. William James aptly called it "the stream of thought, of consciousness, or of subjective life." How can we reconcile these two impressions?

Before tackling that particular problem, consider the role of consciousness in our perception of time, or better, duration. For this purpose, I shall adopt the theory of time duration proposed by Ornstein.[36] His review relates the time experience to "the mechanisms of attention, coding, and storage" (p. 48). Ornstein's central thesis is that storage size is the basis for the "construction of the duration of an interval." The notion of storage size derives directly from recent organizational theory that emphasizes the compact organization of information in memory and experience. The more different unrelated units the greater the storage size, the more highly organized the units, objects, or events are, the fewer are the units or chunks and the smaller is the storage size. As storage size of the material in consciousness increases, the duration experience lengthens. What changes storage size are increases or decreases in the amount of information received, changes in the coding or chunking of input, or, as Ornstein has shown experimentally, influencing the memory of the interval after it has passed. As Ornstein summarized in a later book "the more organized the memory … the shorter the experience of duration."[37]

Generally, then, the experience of duration (in consciousness) is one possible construction drawing on immediately pressing factors (such as attentiveness) but primarily on our stored long-term memory. Duration is constructed — first in the momentary consciousness, and second in the retrieval of events and codes that are recalled during the "construction" of a past interval. The contents of consciousness thus determine the experience of duration. Restricting these contents shortens duration, expanding them, for example, by increasing the complexity of an experience lengthens duration. Vigilance, which increases expectancy of some event, lengthens duration; Ornstein uses the example of the "watched pot." On the other hand, condensing some experience into a very brief code ("I made breakfast") condenses the duration. Ornstein notes, as have others, that our Western linear mode of constructing duration is not the only mode and that present centeredness is not only possible but, in fact, the mode for other cultures than ours. The concatenation of limited conscious capacity, on the one hand, and the same consciousness serving as a vehicle for constructing experience of duration, on the other, brings us back to the disjunction between discrete consciousness and the flow of consciousness.

There is in principle no objection to constructing a flow model of consciousness out of the discrete units of attention or consciousness. The metaphor that comes to mind is a simplistic view of modern conceptions of light, which may be described either in terms of particles or in terms of waves. Again borrowing from physics, we then may metaphorically speak of the quantum of consciousness on the one hand and the flow of consciousness on the other. Another possible metaphor is that of the illusion of moving pictures that consist of individual frames. Neither metaphor probably does justice to the phenomenon, as no metaphor ever does. In particular, it is likely that instead of individual quanta or frames, the flow of consciousness frequently may involve the successive sampling of materials across a continuous retrieval of connected material from long-term storage. Such a phenomenon would depend on the retrieval strategies being used on long-term storage as well as on the nature of the material being sampled. In the case of consciousness of externally generated events, for example, somebody else's speech, the overlapping moving model may be the most appropriate, whereas in attempting the retrieval of a specific chunk of knowledge, the retrieval may be discontinuous.

Because of the limited capacity characteristics of discrete consciousness, I shall use the figure of speech of the conscious frame. We still carry with us the unsolved problem of the content of that slice of consciousness. For the time being we can only allude to the probability that it involves units or chunks of unitary aggregates of information.

Regardless of one's view of the conscious frame as sampling discrete, overlapping, or continuous elements of mental content or environmental input, our view requires a continuous interchange between long-term storage and the conscious state. In the case of an exclusively internal dialogue between the two, material is brought into consciousness and then returned to long-term storage either in essentially unchanged form or after some operations may have been performed on it while in consciousness. Thus, the memory of a friend brought into consciousness may be combined with a new insight that he resembles a recent acquaintance, and then the information is returned with the new relationship coded with it. Or information from storage is brought (within consciousness) in conjunction with new information currently being processed from the environment, for example, "Joe has grown a beard" and then returned to storage newly coded. Many experimental studies of memory require exactly this retrieval from storage and combination, in consciousness, with new information, such as that the word belongs to a particular list or category, or occurs at a particular serial position. I should note, of course, that the distinction between internal and external information is not a very clean one. Clearly, external events do not enter into consciousness as "pure" perceptions, rather they are coded and identified in terms of existing preattentive structures before they enter consciousness.

In general this position joins the long tradition of cognitive and phenomenological psychologists in asserting the importance of the role of consciousness in developing knowledge of oneself and the environment. I do not think that consciousness is primary or sufficient; it is one mode of processing. Just because some evaluation or knowledge does not enter consciousness does not permit a pejorative evaluation of such "automatic" or "unconscious" processing.

Conscious stopping

One special reason why the view of the conscious frame is useful is that it permits a consideration of the special conditions when the flow of consciousness stops, single frames enter into consciousness, and remain there. Experimental psychologists have paid some attention to this phenomenon, as in the concept of maintaining or primary rehearsal, in which material is repeated but does not enter into long-term storage.[38] However, the major source of knowledge of this phenomenon comes from esoteric psychologies and meditative methods.

The best objective presentation of these methods is once again provided by Ornstein.[39] He reviews meditation techniques dispassionately and positively. However, in reading Ornstein's description of these methods, a recurrent theme may be discerned. The achievement of the special kinds of conscious states that are claimed to occur seem to depend, without exception, on the unique attempt to stop the flow of ordinary consciousness — to concentrate on the frame, to hold it fixed in the focus of consciousness. The very difficulty of achieving the initial, apparently trivial, exercises of these techniques suggest the difficulty of stopping the flow. It requires total attention to a single, restricted set of limited thoughts or perceptions. In Zen, the exercises start with counting breaths, and then go on to concentrate on the process of breathing. Yogic meditation uses the mantra, "sonorous, flowing words which repeat easily." Some of the Sufi practices are seen as an "exercise for the brain based on repetition." The Christian mystic St. John of the Cross says: "Of all these forms and manners of knowledge the soul must strip and void itself and it must strive to lose the imaginary apprehension of them, so that there may be left in it no kind of impression of knowledge, nor trace of thought... This cannot happen unless the memory can be annihilated in all its forms, ..."[40] Or, as Ornstein points out, many prayers are monotonous, repetitive chants. In summary, "[The] common element in these diverse practices seems to be the active restriction of awareness to one single, unchanging process, and the withdrawal of attention from ordinary thought" (p. 122). Again: "The specific object used for meditation is much less important than the maintenance of the object as the single focus of awareness during a long period of time ..."(p. 122).

I suggest that the "object of the single focus" must be no more than a frame of consciousness, that in fact it is restricted by the very limits that the limited capacity mechanism has been shown to exhibit. One could not mediate on an event that, at first, contains more than five to seven chunks. The observations that Ornstein and many others have reported suggest that it is in fact possible to stop the flow of consciousness to keep a single frame of consciousness in focus for extended periods of time. However, such an experience should in fact be a very different form of consciousness; the normal form is the flow. We thus become aware of this new consciousness, though only after the extensive practice it requires. However, we must also experience a very different content of consciousness. Given that the single "object" is held in consciousness, many and different aspects of it then may be discovered.

Consider the possibility that at first any such object consists of several related qualities (or chunks). Presumably as these various attributes are related one to the other, the new relations form a more compact perception; the number of chunks, as it were, is reduced. In turn, this opens up the possibility of new chunks or attributes entering into the single frame. New relationships are discovered and again coalesce. Under these circumstances we may go through a process of structuring and restructuring, of discovering aspects of objects or events that would not normally be available to the flow of consciousness. Once this ability has been achieved, one should, in principle, be able to use the special consciousness to stop the flow of events, examine new nuances, and then continue. Thus, a limited set of attributes within a single frame is available at first; then new aspects enter and old ones drop away. The complexities of a rose, a face, or a cake "become conscious." This seems, in fact, to be taking place in what Ornstein calls the "opening up" of awareness, which follows the "turning off" phase and which provides the individual with a different state of comprehension of ongoing actions and events. Again, to quote Ornstein: "The concentrative form turns off the normal mode of operation and allows a sensitivity to subtle stimuli which often go unnoticed in the normal mode... It also produces an aftereffect of 'fresh' perception when the practitioner returns to his usual surroundings".[41] What I wish to add to Ornstein's insightful discussion is the possibility that modern psychology may define the process wherein this attentiveness occurs and also the processes which generate new perceptions and sensitivities. Meditative techniques provide us, in this fashion, with new insights into a mechanism that otherwise seems rather mundane and restrictive. There need not be anything mysterious about meditation, nor anything pedestrian about an information processing analysis of consciousness.

The enriching of knowledge though meditative experiences or, as we might call it, conscious stopping, should be put into the proper context of the ordinary, normal means of enriching experience. Without doubt, we enrich our experience and knowledge about the world around us without resorting to meditation. We can, without special preparation, perceive new facets about the world, about other people, even about ourselves as we gain new perspectives, new ways of structuring our experience. One of the main differences between the normal and the meditative enrichment is that the former deals with an open system, the latter deals with a closed one. Our enrichment in knowledge and appreciation of a lover, a novel, a science, an occupation occurs always in new contexts, sometimes widely different, sometimes only minutely so. However, the relationship between the object or event and ourselves is changed continuously by our mutual relations with the rest of the world. The new information is, in a way, always acquired in new contexts. What seems to distinguish this usual accretion from the meditative one is that the latter is a closed system; we are restricted to those relationships among qualities and attributes that are given in that object or situation. This restriction of possible relations presumably provides not only the illusion but possibly also the reality of depth of perception which the special experience provides. In contrast, artists and scientists, for example, apparently achieve the same depth of perception of special objects or events without the meditative experience. Ornstein's notion that the experience of duration is constructed, based on the storage size of the cognitive structures that constitute an interval, may be applied directly to the flow and frame aspects of consciousness. In the open-system flow, time experience is constructed across frames out of cognitive structures that will, to varying degrees, occupy the capacity of the limited-capacity frame. Consider listening to a lecture on difficult, but interesting material. As the speaker proceeds, information is transmitted at a great rate, taking up the full capacity of each frame of consciousness. In Ornstein's terms, storage of information is near a maximum. As a result, the duration experience increases. In contrast, the redundant speaker makes fewer demands on each frame, the very ability to approach a difficult subject slowly and cumulatively permits us to use less of the full capacity of the frame, or, as another possibility, the capacity is filled less frequently in physical time and fewer frames are expended. In any case, the experience of duration is more extended in the former than in the latter case. It is interesting to speculate that Ornstein's storage metaphor may be directly translated into the frame locution. Since consciousness is necessary for the transfer of information to long-term storage, complex (many chunks and relations) information requires more frames for the transfer function, as does rapidly presented information (more chunks per unit physical time). It appears that the storage metaphor is quite consistent with the frame-flow notion of consciousness. In the latter mode the construction of time depends on the sheer number of frames of consciousness activated or utilized during a specified interval. Parenthetically this position also indicates the independence of the conscious frame from physical time. The specious present, the limited-capacity mechanism, does not have a time constant. Frames are replaced under a variety of conditions, all of which seem to depend on using up their capacity, a new perceptual dimension, another class of stimulation, a sudden demand for focusing (attention), and many others will demand a shift to another content of consciousness, which is perceived as another moment of consciousness.

Finally, we may note the rather drastic changes in time perception that take place as a result of meditative experience. Given that the flow of frames is radically altered, one would naturally expect a similar and unusual change in duration experiences. The direction can be either way. Holding a single unit of consciousness and impeding the flow may collapse the duration experience, whereas the eventual ability to manipulate the flow of consciousness may change the usual duration experience with its apparently rather constant rate of change into a more variable ebb and flow of "short" and "long" durations. Instead of the flow of frames during normal states, during meditation the change from one conscious content to another occurs infrequently in physical time. The slow changes in perceptual structures which I suggested earlier for the meditative phase thus produce unusual duration experiences.

It is intriguing to speculate that the action of hallucinogenic or "mind-expanding" drugs has a similar locus and effect. Changes in perceptual processes coexist with changes in the experience of duration. It has been argued that these drugs often produce in the instant the experiences that meditative methods generate with extensive practice. It is possible that some drugs in fact slow the flow of conscious frames, and that some of the lasting effects of these drugs may be due to structural changes in control of the flow of consciousness. [*It is regrettable that in recent years hardly anybody (including me) has paid any attention to the special states of consciousness in trying to understand the nature of conscious experience*]

Conclusion

The concept of consciousness was abandoned as a proper object of experimental study some 60 years [*Now 85 years*] ago. The reasons were manifold. The introspective method erred in assuming that consciousness could be made the datum of psychology or that verbal report was a royal road to its exploration. The failure of introspection both engendered behaviorism and failed to provide any viable alternatives. Others, like the Gestalt school and the French and English enclaves, successfully defended their view of the conscious organism, but had, for theoretical reasons, little ground to mount a major analytic attack. The return of American psychology to a theory-rich as well as experimentally rigorous stance has given us the opportunity to develop the proper theoretical tools to return consciousness to its proper place in a theory of thought, mind, and actions. Most of the early steps that have been taken have been necessarily preliminary models and developments of experimental methods. My primary aim in these pages has been to try to point to the directions that these preliminary steps are taking. Granted that this has been a personal view at the current stage, it will have been successful if it generates discussion and investigation and, eventually, theory, which will define and specify the role that consciousness plays in man's transactions with his world. [*So much for testing the waters, and as I was writing the chapter it became obvious that it should become part of my 1975 book* Mind and Emotion *that I was writing at the same time. Essentially unchanged it became Chapter 3 of that book*].

That was the beginning and there followed some 16 papers, chapters and books in which the topic was taken up again, arguments repeated and renewed, new thoughts adopted. In 1996 I summarized this journey and will not repeat the serial account here.[42] In fact, except for most of the parenthetically amended material I believe that much of the foregoing will still stand today. I now start with an evolutionary hypothesis which serves as a framework for the preceding speculations and also for what follows.

Chapter 2

An evolutionary scenario as a framework for consciousness

I start with some speculation and a preliminary evolutionary scenario. One usually leaves evolutionary speculations to the end of a discussion of a phenomenon. However, as my exploration of conscious phenomena crystallized I became increasingly aware of the need for a unifying set of principles — a theory if you will — from which these various observations would follow. And the evolutionary story that I tell constitutes that kind of a framework.

The background

The psychology of the 19th century was committed to the notion that its subject matter was the contents of consciousness. Even though doubts were raised that there may be interesting things going on unconsciously,[43] it was not until Freud opened the doors of the dynamic unconscious and the Würzburg group[44] inferred the cognitive unconscious that the dominance of the conscious began to ebb. Obviously important processes were going on in the absence of conscious access, as Freud and the Würzburgers demonstrated, the behaviorists implied, and the Gestaltists asserted. With the more recent emergence of a new theoretical psychology (so called cognitive psychology) which clearly asserted at first that most of the interesting action was going on at the unconscious (theoretical?) level, consciousness was still rather tentatively approached. But in the 1970s there started a real interested in the functions and structure of consciousness, soon joined by philosophers in search of a juicy topic. Today the relation between unconscious and conscious processes has achieved what seems an appropriate balance — both are important. I next elaborate a part of this history.[45]

William James looked at consciousness as primarily a representation of self and invoked the self as participating in most conscious functions. He resisted analytic attempts at breaking down the conscious experience; he was after all an advocate of the pan-psychic that imbued all natural phenomena with some conscious aspects. Wilhelm Wundt, the experimentalist, wanted to experiment, to analyze the conscious experience, and built his first laboratory on such a program. By the end of the century however Wundt, despite his commitment to the analysis of sensations, had started to worry about the deleterious drive toward analysing and "deconstructing" the contents of consciousness, and in fact Titchener — claiming in part Wundt's mantle in America — undertook a structural analysis of the components of consciousness. He failed because his method of introspection tended to find the contents that he told his subjects to look for. The approach was put to rest by the functionalists, led by Angell, Carr and others, who had listened to the call for evolutionary analyses and who wanted to know about the evolution of the mind and were interested in observables and their function. In Germany the Wundtian position was succeeded by the Gestaltists, who argued that analysis destroys the very basis of experience and perception, which must consider the experiential whole against the appropriate background. That was where we were when the behaviorist — classical American and Puritan — arrived on the scene and denied any utility or function to consciousness, it being at best subjective and unobservable, at worst just epiphenomenal. Though note that Skinner, the bright light on the behaviorist horizon, had no problem talking about private events and their role and function.

The main victim of behaviorism was imaginative theorizing. Under behaviorism it was difficult to assign theoretical mechanisms to the unconscious. Concepts such as habit strength or reflex reserve just did not seem appropriate for unconscious assignment. And by 1953 Boring was able to write: "… The substitution of differential response for the old-fashioned dated existential consciousness does away with immediate experience."[46] And it was not until the 1970s that psychologists were able to overcome the fear of talking about consciousness.

Talking about consciousness as a special phenomenon became relevant by the beginning of the 20th century when the unconscious had been generally accepted, i.e., that many mental processes took place out of the reach of conscious access. The process started in earnest with von Hartmann, was taken up by Freud, and was confirmed for experimental psychology by the Würzburgers' discovery of "imageless thought" and implicitly by organizing principles of the Gestalt psychologists. The "discovery" of the unconscious — the postulation of the representation of all actions and memories, choices and perceptions — made possible the notion that there was a theoretical/psychological mediating level between physiology and experience and a psychological language was developed by the turn of the century. This made possible talking about nonconscious, including theoretical, phenomena without having to take refuge in one's ignorance of brain mechanisms. Later it would mean that psychological discovery would make possible a specification of what kind and manner of brain mechanisms one should look for. However once these levels of analysis were established it seemed to appropriate to ask how these different levels of mental operation arose. Some few hardy souls ventured into an analysis of possible evolutionary mechanisms that gave rise to the complexities of the mental system.[47]

Some possible evolutionary mechanisms concerned with consciousness

For some 25 years I have argued that consciousness is, in part, the final way-station of the reduction of information from the blooming confusion of the external world reduced by the limitations of the sensory organs, then by the transduction devices from the peripheral organs, and further by the systematic reduction in the central nervous system to the final limited information that is our daily consciousness. The reduction from the potential information available in the world to the final bit of conscious knowledge is of several orders of magnitude. Unaided we know very little about our world.

The adaptive need for and selection of some systematic reduction of information occurred at some time when the complexity of tasks to be accomplished and information to be monitored became sufficiently demanding. The "conscious" reduction may have emerged with respect to only one or some part of the functions of consciousness described here. Subsequently, and in a homologous fashion, the system was adopted for other functions. We still develop consciousness — ontogenetically — as it is needed and made possible by the requisite underlying structures. Gould has made a similar argument that important (conscious) cognitive functions are not an orderly consequence of biological improvement, but rather the fortuitous consequence of neural complexity evolved for other reasons. Specifically "as a result of larger size, and the neural density and connectivity thus imparted, human brains could perform an immense range of functions quite unrelated to the original reasons for increase in bulk."[48]

I will not repeat in detail the several arguments in Chapter 1 for the adaptiveness of consciousness, particularly in its function of facilitating comparing and planning. However, in respect to some of the important functions of consciousness, how does consciousness contribute to the procreative advantages of the conscious organism?

The serial and limited capacity aspects contribute to probabilities of survival and selection by making decisions both quicker and more relevant to the current situation. An organism that is not overwhelmed by too many alternatives, that is able to consider the relevant ones in an orderly fashion one at a time is more likely to survive (and produce offspring) than one that may be panicked by the rush of possible actions. The notion that we make decisions on the basis of limited information has been discussed and demonstrated by Gigerenzer and his co-workers.[49] They have, for example, argued that inferences are made with limited time and knowledge available, using relatively simple perceptual and choice mechanisms. Limited and serial processing would be quite consistent with this approach.

In addition to limiting immediate capacity and presenting information in a serial fashion, these "conscious" mechanisms also sometimes have another important characteristic — their subjective, qualia-like aspect. I will return to the emergence of subjective consciousness, for now I want to stress that seriality and capacity limitation may occur without subjectivity, but that subjectivity is regnant in such areas as planning, comparison and evaluation.

The advantage of limited capacity is particularly obvious in the context of what I have called the "troubleshooting" function of consciousness. When habitual actions fail it is important to be able to find substitute actions quickly, and one of the functions of consciousness is to bring into awareness situations in which automatic actions fail or are disrupted. Claparède has called this the law of awareness.[50]

The notion that consciousness permits differential selection and use of potential actions and thoughts is common to most current conceptions, including notions of intentionality. However, I emphasize the fact that a limited serial system (regardless of phenomenal subjectivity) cannot be limited to human beings. Seriality and limitation are also necessary to understand the survival needs of other animals. Put another way, serial and limited access to unconscious, unactivated representation is characteristic of human beings by direct observation and implicitly operating in other animals as well. But what are their uses, if not an improvement in the struggle for survival?

My point of view does not view consciousness as an all-or-none phenomenon, i.e., either you have "it" or you don't. Rather it emerges in response to the demands of processing in special domains and in different domains at different times. Consciousness may or may not be a function exclusive to human beings, and — more important — it did not suddenly, or recently come into existence. Such a view is in direct contrast to philosophers and psychologists who give it a uniquely human flavor, circumscribed by language and human mentality. In particular it denies the claims of Julian Jaynes that consciousness emerged some few thousand years ago.[51]

I assume that current conscious contents are constructed by a higher order schema or structure that accesses usually two or more lower structures and integrates them into a single conscious construction that responds to the requirements of the moment. That assumption is supported by the inability of amnesic patients to engage in such novel constructions (see Chapter 5 on amnesia as a disease of consciousness) and by some of Marcel's work on the construction of perceptual phenomena. One of the consequences of such a position is that "consciousness" is not a given characteristic of an individual person or animal, but rather that the individual has the potential of constructing a conscious content if and only if some mental structure or need are available that construct a particular conscious content at any given moment. Thus, people are not and cannot be conscious of just anything in their environments or in their psychic armamentarium, but rather that one may become conscious of specific kinds of events in one's internal or external environment. Which kinds of events that includes depends on the prior experience one has had with the phenomena and experiences in question. This accounts, for example, for painters and musicians being able to perceive (consciously) aspects of art and music that the untrained eye and ear does not perceive. Prior experience with the constituents, and some initial construction, need for, and knowledge about relevant higher order structures are necessary. In other words, the development of consciousness about certain objects and events may be a slow and cumulative process.

The most striking representation in consciousness, of course, is the representation of the self, of the structures and schemas that represent knowledge of the person that we are, our needs and wishes, fears and hopes. This ability to be aware of ourselves is not a separate characteristic developed or given at some blinding point in time, but rather it is one other — and overwhelmingly persuasive — result of the development of cognition and consciousness. As I will argue again later, the self is not some unusual structure but the most developed of all the schemas that we construct as we interact with the world and that inform our knowledge (our cognitions) of our external and internal environment. Schemas are the most important set of structures in the construction of knowledge. Other mental structures, some available to consciousness, others not, represent grammars, relations among unidimensional representations, and-, if-, and or-connections and any other relational building material in our mental armamentarium.

This kind of approach may also be useful in understanding the development of consciousness in the young child. Thus, we would not expect that an infant suddenly becomes conscious of its entire world, but rather that the ability to construct conscious contents will depend on the developing experience with the surrounds. For example, one would expect the child to form early consciousnesses about its caretakers, about hunger management, and so forth. On the other hand, consciousness about language would take quite some time until specific initial structures are developed which then may become the constituents of higher order structures that construct conscious knowledge about the use and structure of language. Thus, the metalinguistic abilities of children, i.e., what it is that the child knows about language that the spider does not know about its web will emerge with the development and mastery of language.[52]

Next, consider the problem of animal consciousness. It may not be the case that mammals are either conscious or not, but rather that the ability to construct conscious contents has developed somewhere within the mammalian groups, but the richness and extent of consciousness depends on the richness and extent of their underlying cognitive structures that encode and structure their ability to know and deal with the world. Cognitively relatively sophisticated animals, such as the primates, will have a more extensive conscious apparatus than less sophisticated animals such as rodents. The question may be not be whether the animal is conscious but rather what the limited number of events and objects are about which it can be conscious.

One precursor of consciousness can be found in the vicarious trials and errors (VTEs) observed in the choice point behavior of nonhuman animals.[53] VTEs consist of the visual sampling of possible choices, sometimes including short forays to one or the other side of the choice point, before the actual choice occurs. Such "sampling" increases the relevant activations of underlying representation when there is no representation in consciousness to perform that function of selective activation. The same kind of behavioral, in contrast to mental, sampling can also be observed in adult humans (e.g., under stress) and in infants. Let me suggest that VTEs are frequently no more than the external signs of spatio-temporal "attention" (see Chapter 5). Such an attentional phenomenon frequently gives rise to the attribution of intentionality and consciousness to the attending organism. Attention to objects and space-time events is by itself not evidence for a conscious organism.

These considerations led to a minimalist conjecture and some interesting problems. A minimal number of assumptions and requirements does justice to the known functions of consciousness. Can we entertain an understanding of conscious phenomena by considering only three basic functions of consciousness? I stress these three functions because they seem to be unarguably part of our conscious apparatus. The obviousness of these three postulates has not, however, always struck other explorers of the conscious.

> Three obvious characteristics of consciousness:
> a. The selective/constructive representation of unconscious structures relevant to current concerns.
> b. The conversion from a parallel and vast unconscious to a serial and limited representation that is frequently subjectively conscious.
> c. The selective activation (priming) by conscious representations that changes the unconscious landscape by producing new privileged structures (the feedback function of consciousness which I discuss below).

All of these characteristics are amenable to empirical investigations, and in the end the question is whether these minimalist assumptions are adequate to handle the most obvious or inferred functions of consciousness. Given these three, what else is needed, and is it consistent with these assumptions? Or is there another core of assumptions that might command assent from a large number of theorists. Until that question can be settled (or even asked?), there are a number of specific questions which deserve further investigation.

Consciousness and short-term memory (STM)

The distinction between short-term and long-term memory goes back at least to the beginnings of the information processing movement. Is it not about time that we bring STM into line with what we know about consciousness?

If in STM we "retrieve" only whatever consciousness will "hold," then we are limited to retrieving some 5+/– items. The limitation is the same for STM and limited capacity consciousness, both of which are restricted to a single organized set with about 5 discernable constituent attributes, features, items, etc. William James coined the term "primary memory" to designate this information that is currently available in consciousness. But any operation on the limited material held in consciousness will further activate and bound that material, providing a small set of highly activated preconscious representations. Thus STM consists of "primary", currently conscious, contents and additional material that is very easily retrieved because it is the product of these short term retrievals and activations. In addition items "in" STM may have been elaborated or merely activated, a difference that may determine their rate of decay or accessibility.[54]

Why is the limited capacity what it is?
Whether one wishes to define the limited capacity as 3 or 5 or 7 items/chunks, some such magnitude has been accepted ever since George Miller's seminal paper in 1956 on the "magical number." Of all the possible genetic determinants of human cognition, the one that defines the limited capacity of consciousness seems to demand more serious attention than some of the more extravagant evolutionary conjectures that circulate these days. It seems intuitively reasonable that the number needs to be more than 2 and probably less than 10 if fast decision processes on a reasonable number of alternatives are required for survival. But why the number we've got?

How do we determine conscious contents?
Nearly thirty years ago Adrian noted that psychology's "uncertainty principle" may well be the fact that the very interrogation of conscious contents may alter these contents.[55] Can we circumvent this problem? What alternatives, such as Dennett's heterophenomenology,[56] are available?

What would we be like if we were not conscious? Essentially I claim that consciousness lets us experience an ordered and selective stream of thoughts and actions that in turn direct subsequent thought and action. What would happen if there were no conversion to serial limited consciousness? Assume that the *how* of consciousness remains the same but that there is no limitation of capacity. We would be overwhelmed by parallel-produced thoughts and possible actions, close to indiscriminately cascading in our consciousness. If we then also relaxed the seriality requirement, we would be conscious of all our possible thought all at once — we would know everything about ourselves and all out past experiences contemporaneously. But I know of only one being for whom such possibilities are claimed, and therefore in the absence of these limitation and seriality mechanism we would be God-like — or close to madness.

So much for the rather sketchy outlines of what consciousness "does." I will elaborate many of these points in later chapters, but for now I want to move to the quasi-theory that I trust will motivate much of the rest of this book. I call it a "quasi"-theory because whereas it is a statement of certain *a priori* assumptions about consciousness it is not a determinedly effective system for making testable predictions.

An evolutionary scenario

I introduce a possible evolutionary scenario in three steps. The main reason is that it is unlikely that the three components of consciousness — Seriality, limited capacity, and subjectivity — would be achieved in one fell swoop. Responsible evolutionary theory since Darwin has insisted on the slow accumulation of complex traits. And that must be true of consciousness as it is of the human eye, birds' wings, language (*pace* Chomsky) and many other complex adaptations.

Consider a complex organism — possibly an early mammal or one of its ancestors — where the nervous system has become so complex that the information processing mind is impeded by the simultaneous assault from a variety of different, but relevant, contenders for actions and execution.[57] Early in its history the organism had a rather limited repertory to deal with either threats or attractants in its environment. It might, for example, be able to run away or stay put. As its mental and behavioral repertory becomes more complex, as its evolution provides a richer repertory of possible actions, the organism may have acquired a number of different ways of dealing with its environment. Consider that the organism now may, in response to a predator, run, fight, dissimulate, bargain etc. And when confronted by a predator all or many of these possible actions contend for execution. In many cases the resultant competition among many different possible actions (arraigned against each other in terms of response strengths, action potential, or whatever) will result in a delay of action — and failure to survive. In the same way food seeking activity, including such activities as pursuing potential foods or collecting edible greenery, may similarly be impeded. Hunted animals are not reached as quickly, potable food is not identified quickly enough.

Along comes blind natural selection. At some time a mutation appears which produces a very simple alternative outcome. It reduces the N possible outcome to a random sample of n possibilities, where n is one half or some other fraction of N, as long as the result is that when confronted by a predator, the individual animal will have significantly fewer actions contending for execution. Similarly when foraging or hunting fewer alternatives will vie for execution. On average, the lucky individual endowed with the new mechanism will have a greater chance of survival than its progenitor who needed to consider N alternatives, and the same advantages will be available to its offspring. A necessary characteristic of this selective process is that the alternatives do not — as the unconscious ones are likely to do — appear all at once, but rather occur serially; they compete without overshadowing each other. After some reasonably long time we have a new line of the species in question with a better chance of survival (and therefore procreation) — the mutation is clearly adaptive.

However, there is still the probability that among the actions that are selected by the new mechanism the best possible action — the most likely to succeed in the animal/predator or food seeking scenarios — will not be selected. The selection of a small set out of the larger one is at this point random. It is better than having all the possible actions contending, but it certainly is susceptible to improvement.

Millennia go by and another mutation occurs — that one acts on the random selection, and instead of making it random it selects the ones most likely to succeed. It is not obvious how that selection occurs, though a number of possible criteria are possible. The new mutation may function to select the action that in the past has been most successful, or one that best "fits" the circumstances (there is clear running room for escape or for reaching one's prey), or the predator or prey are perceived to be weak (and therefore fighting is possible), etc. In short, the selection now is not just random but actually selects the best possible contenders, the ones most relevant and important to the current situation. This optimality choice is of course a function of the individual organism's experience and may not always be the objectively best choice.

I pause to note that these two steps are introduced only because it seems more reasonable that the random selection preceded the "relevant" selection; nothing, except the simplicity of evolution, would prevent the two steps to have occurred in a single mutational leap. Also, the examples I used are only a few where these mechanisms might work — choice of proper (nonpoisonous) foods, competition with member of one's group, choice of sleeping location etc. all might benefit at one time or another from selection by the improved mechanism.

I argue that this preferential selection of possible actions is what constitutes the initial steps toward subjective consciousness. It affects a variety of different so-called "functions" of consciousness described above and in Chapter 1. It handles such things as trouble shooting and choice behavior that cover a large range of consciously influenced actions.

How about the "special problem of consciousness" — its subjective and apparent "conscious" function, its delivery of the troublesome qualia. I suggest that the qualia aspect, the subjective conscious experience may have come along as an initially fortuitous aspect of one of the two (or more) mutational moves.

Natural selection is blind, if a mutation works it cares little of what noninterfering or nonlethal characteristics it brings with it. The scenario I present works up to a point with or without qualia, it just so happens that the qualia — the very "conscious" aspect of the change — may have been brought along with the adaptive mutation. The result is not unimportant or causally irrelevant. As the organismic carrier of the new mutations became more complex, more intelligent, more adapted to using and changing their environment and doing such marvellous things as inventing language, they learned to use this experiential, subjective aspect of the selection process. By steps beyond my power to imagine, the experiential aspect of this "consciousness" became important in the individual and interactive life of human beings (and possibly some other animals) to the point where the choice mechanisms and the experience of being conscious became independently important and causally effective. Among the functions that developed out of this subjectivity were the ability to compare contents of different "conscious" strands, of establishing desirable relations among thoughts and actions and of discovering some of these relations. I have described some of these possible functions of subjective experiences at greater length in Chapter 1, including the testing of short and long term plans, storage and retrieval of memories, social cooperation, and troubleshooting the failure of unconscious actions.

It is the realization of the manifold adaptive uses of subjective consciousness that made it difficult to chose which of them may have been the initial target of natural selection. That was one reason that motivates my suggestion about the fortuitous appearance of subjective consciousness, which then — over time — developed its various adaptive functions.

It should be emphasized however that many functions of consciousness depend primarily, if not solely, on the initial seriation and limitation of thought and actions. For example, the acquisition of new behaviors — "learning" in the old dictionary of psychology — can take place with or without subjectivity. Without it it is best represented by the conditioning and reinforcement models of the more imaginative behaviorists. No consciousness is necessary for the juxtaposition of mental content to co-occur with a reinforcing event, for example. On the other hand, the acquisition of simple and complex knowledge (e.g., "x is a y") requires understanding (having subjectively present) the meaning of the participating representations. In other words, without subjectivity this consciousness model accommodates simple learning, with subjectivity it makes possible cognitive (informational) learning.

Some of the functions of consciousness discussed in Chapter 1 and in this chapter may well have been generated by the use of these exaptive characteristics associated fortuitously with one or the other of the adaptive mutations.[58] Thus the reduction of alternatives may have been accompanied by the qualia characteristics which was initially of no particular adaptive use but became so later.

One of the arguments for the extraneous character of the addition of qualia-like subjective experience is that much of what a serial, limited capacity consciousness can do in terms of improving decision processes, it can do without subjective consciousness. It would be easy to imagine an animal that acts on the most adaptive (life preserving and enhancing) possible actions without being "conscious" of these alternatives.[59] But these adaptive improvements are what are usually called conscious actions and experiences. Even in humans the absence of qualia-consciousness does not prevent adequate problem solving behavior. The well known case of H. M. with an extremely dense amnesia is a case in point.[60] For example, when he was presented repeatedly with the Towers of Hanoi puzzle he saw the puzzle each time as something never encountered before, but then he solved it more rapidly each time, starting off at the level of competence more or less where he left off the last time. Without qualia-conscious access to his previous successes the limiting aspects of consciousness still narrowed his choices to ones not excluded by prior experience.

The exaptive character of subjective qualia-like experience may have been with animals like us for a very long time and during that time various aspects of the experiential quality of selected mental actions, memories etc. became available for interactive changes in our mental apparatus and — presumably in coaction with other mutations — generated the new conscious individual.

Just as the evolution of the human hand produced magical functions such as painting and writing far beyond the original evolutionary outcome, so has consciousness had several very useful consequences. In contrast to other treatments I do not put special emphasis on the functioning of sensory *qualia.* I do not believe that there is a special problem of *sensory qualia.* It has been asserted that "*qualia* are the unique properties that accompany our perception like the 'redness of red'." But the problem of consciousness is the same for all states of the brain that lead to/are correlated with/cause some conscious state, including "the sixness of 2 times 3" and the "presidentialness of George Washington." Sensory experiences are just a subset of these phenomena, not a special problem. The remaining open question is the mechanism of subjective consciousness, and I assume that sometime in the future we will understand how this happens.

I note that the mechanisms I discussed may have been such that some random selection mechanisms are still active and that some of the choice mechanisms do not carry "qualia" with them. Thus at times we can make non optimal choices and even some of which we are not "conscious." At the risk of offending the more romantic viewers of the human condition, I remind the reader that some (many?) human actions are unconscious, and therefore often seen as unwilled or automatic.

Since I believe that both the limited and serial quality of consciousness and its subjective aspects are equally important in the functioning of the whole, it is crucial to refer to the two components differently when referring to one or the other function. "Qualia"/subjective consciousness is dependent on the serial/limited precursors. In other words the precursors are necessary for consciousness to occur, but obviously not sufficient. Conversely the limited/serial reduction can result in action without consciousness being invoked at all. Thus it is not possible to speak of conscious events without taking into account the essential precursors that limit and arrange the conscious contents.

More important is the fact that whereas attentional mechanisms may be responsible for selecting occasions and events that are relevant and important to the current situation, attention is not a necessary precursor of consciousness. In fact, nonattentional processes, particularly when the individual is in a passive attitude or state, produce large numbers of interesting conscious states. These will be discussed in Chapter 5.

I will have occasion later to discuss other special cases of access to consciousness. One of them is the experience of pain — one of the most obvious emergency mechanisms of the animal body — which is by definition "important" and relevant to the present situation and will under the appropriate circumstance receive priority access to conscious expression. The other is in a sense the very opposite, the occasions when the limited capacity of consciousness is not fully utilized.

I have to this point argued that subjective consciousness was probably a fortuitous event. My main reason is that the wonderful tricks that subjective consciousness makes possible seem to be later developments of the basic phenomenon, just as the five-fingered hand did not evolve with handwriting as its "goal," or language for poetry, feet for dancing, and so forth. From something as basic as the juxtaposition of possible alternatives in decision processes, to the confrontation with the unexpected, to the exquisite conscious skill of writing poems or composing music, the subjective consciousness developed important functions. I particularly like what might be the most important juxtaposition between truth and lie illustrated by the Russian poet's Joseph

Brodsky's "the real history of consciousness starts with one's first lie."

The initial characteristic of subjective consciousness surely did not include all of these ways of taking advantage of it subjectivity and contrasting skills. However, my argument does not depend on the exaptive nature of consciousness. It could have performed some initially adaptive functions and therefore was a useful mutation rather than a fortuitous event. I prefer one of these alternatives, but they are not contradictory in principle — either could have been the case.

A special case of exaptation is demonstrated by spandrels, a term adopted by Gould and Lewontin[61] from architecture. Originally spandrels referred to the fortuitous occurrence of structures as a result of other functional ones, as in the case of triangles formed by interacting arches. In evolutionary biology the spandrel refers to the fortuitous effect of some adaptation(s). In the course of biological evolution these accidental products may eventually serve some useful purpose. In this sense the original evolutionary steps in the emergence of consciousness described above may have produced the byproduct of a qualia spandrel which eventually becomes useful and functional.

My argument does not imply, as has been posited by some epiphenomenalists, that consciousness is not adaptive. On the contrary I believe that with further evolutionary development of the initially fortuitous qualia consciousness a variety of forms of its eventual functions have become adaptive and important in the life of the species. The use of qualia consciousness in planning, memory, perception, and others, is adaptive and of great importance in dealing with the world the species inhabits. My argument that subjective consciousness might well be exaptive is not crucial; the development could have been the result of an adaptive selection. I find it difficult, though, to imagine how some single initially adaptive aspect of consciousness would have been selected and produced reproductive fitness.

Whether or not qualia are normal adaptations, exaptive accidents, or even spandrels, the quest for their underlying physiology is of course an important and interesting adventure. And whether some such mechanisms as Crick and Koch's[62] or one of many other possibilities are the underlying material bases will, however, be relatively independent of the function and use of conscious mental events.

On the frequently asked question about the possibility of consciousness in nonterrestrial or artificial life forms, the present approach suggests that similarities with humans will arise if the adaptation is one of improved, optimal choices and that it may have little to do with the presence or reporting of qualia.

Chapter 3

The construction of conscious contents

Constructivism: The emergence of complex structures and experiences

What fascinates us about organisms is their complexity, their ability to engage in complex thought and actions and — in the case of humans at least — to have accompanying subjective experiences. Whence come these complexities? Do they spring full blown into existence like Athena from the brow of Zeus, or are they carefully assembled with Lego-like components? I argue, positively biased for evolution and negatively against phenomenology, that an assembly approach, a constructivism is the only reasonable interpretation,

The argument based on evolutionary theory goes back to Darwin's own hard fight against those of his contemporaries who wanted the complex behavioral and physical skills of humans and other animals to be found in the continuous creation of new species and beings. The argument was that each new complex behavior or animal was either created by the Almighty or the result of evolutionary selection — depending how far along the road to science one had come. Modern evolutionary views usually (but not always) continue the constructivist approach. Thus Kitcher has argued for evolutionary processes that generate proximal development rather than creating complex distal events and actions.[63] S. J. Gould in general, and in coining the phrase exaptation, has stressed the importance of initially unrelated evolutionary events in the eventual construction of useful structures. The remnants of the opposition can be found in the romanticism of Noam Chomsky and others in the invocation of sudden jumps in human abilities and ingenuities. Unfortunately many of these magical qualities have been endorsed by psychologists, often based on flawed investigations of human genetics.[64] Do we want to invoke evolution brought about by the blind watchmaker or by the modern equivalent of god imagining the ready made components of the world and humanity?

My phenomenological argument is a negative one. It accepts the nature of common experience which presents complex thoughts, memories etc. as singular unified experiences. But that phenomenal experience has sometimes entrapped psychologists. Historically, up to the end of the 19th century the patent contents of consciousness were considered to be the building blocks of the mind and our experience. It was not until the turn of the century that notions of the unconscious were taken seriously. Phenomenal conscious experience receded as the unanalyzable essence of psychology, and theoretical and unconscious entities were brought into play for an explanation of human psychology. One argument against a phenomenological basis for human psychology is the current consensus that conscious phenomena represent only a small part of our mental apparatus.

Before discussing specific problems of conscious construction I need to describe and discuss a central concept in such a construction — the notion of the schema.

The schema as a building block of consciousness

The notion of the schema has been with us at least since Immanuel Kant who gave us a prototype that is still valid. Consider Kant's description of the schema of a dog as a mental pattern "that can delineate the figure of a four-footed animal in a general manner, without any limitation to any single determinate [i.e., concrete] figure [that] experience, or any image that I can represent … , actually presents."[65] These experiential depositories provide us with the wherewithal to understand, interpret, and perceive our world. A schema is a coherent, i.e., unitary, representation that organizes experience. Schemas are not carbon copies of experience, but abstract representations of experiential regularities. They range from the very concrete, involving the most primitive categorization of perceptual experience, to the very abstract, representing general levels of meaning. Schemas are built up slowly as we experience our world in the course of our interaction with the social and physical environment. I use the term schema to conform with current usage but also to evoke similarities with Bartlett's and Piaget's usage.

Schemas[66] are built up in the course of interaction with the environment. They are available at increasing levels of generality and abstraction. Thus, schemas may represent organized experience ranging from discrete features to general categories. For example, one schema may represent a horse's head, and another one facilitates the perception of a particular animal as a horse because of the concatenation of certain features (variables of a schema) such as a head, a tail, a mane, a certain size, or a range of colors. That same horse is categorized as an animal because of the occurrence of certain defining characteristics of that class of events. The schema is a category of mental structures that organize past experience, that structure our experience and are being structured by it. An exploration by Rumelhart and Ortony provides some of the specifications of schemas:[67]

The schema that is developed as a result of prior experiences with a particular kind of event is not a carbon copy of that event; schemas are abstract representations of environmental regularities. Schemas vary from the most concrete to the most abstract; they are available for the perceptual elements of an event as well as for the abstract representation of its "meaning" or gist. We comprehend events in terms of the schemas they activate, though we have different ways of talking about different kinds of comprehension. For example, perception is "comprehension of sensory input"; one sense of understanding involves comprehension of semantic relations; and some value judgments are based on the comprehension of structural relations. Finally, it should be noted that generic schemas have modal (or even canonic) values of variables. This property responds to the notion of schematic prototypes,[68] which affect the likely congruity of specific instances of objects and events.

Schemas operate interactively, i.e., input from the environment is coded selectively in keeping with the schemas currently operating while that input also selects relevant schemas.[69] Whenever some event in the environment produces "data" for the schematic analysis, the activation process proceeds automatically (and interactively) to the highest (most abstract) relevant schema. At the same time, the activation of a schema also involves the inhibition of other competing schemas. Evidence from the environment activates potential schemas, and active schemas produce an increased readiness for certain evidence and decreased readiness (inhibition) for other evidence. The particular interaction between the contextual environmental evidence and the organism's available schemas constricts perception and conception to specific hypotheses, constructions, and schemas.

Finally, the concept of the schema also provides one approach to some of the problems of "binding." How consciousness is restricted to a particular and circumscribed set of events has been a continuing problem in understanding cognitive processes and their limitation. Harrison has stated it succinctly: "Experientially, our conscious awareness of events, percepts and concepts is smooth and seamless, yet our sensory modalities, and the cognitive system that manipulates their inputs, consist of millions of small independently functioning units. What allows us to bind that fractionated input into a cohesive experience?"[70] The postulation of schemas, built up as a function of experience with events and objects, opens one solution to the problem of binding. Experiences are "seamless" and unitary to the extent that they activate existing and available schemas.

The construction of conscious experience

Given that conscious contents arise out of activated nonconscious depositories of past experience (as well as inherited characteristics of the species) I now move to the question of the manner in which these conscious contents are constructed, how they respond to the needs of the moment, the power of past experience and other factors.

The general approach is one of functionalism — a psychologist's functional approach, which considers the functions and roles that consciousness apparently fills in mental life.[71] I am concerned primarily with consciousness in terms of immediate experience, whether it is of extra- or intra-psychic events or is reflective. The question is why some mental contents appear in that conscious guise. I am concerned with certain functions of human cognition that map on to consciousness — when mental contents tend to display such functions as seriality and limited capacity and are likely to prime underlying representations. I emphasize the following functions of conscious states:

First, consciousness is limited in capacity and occurs serially.

Second, conscious states respond to the current situational and intentional imperatives.

Third, unconscious representations and processes generate all thoughts and processes, whether conscious or not; the unconscious is where the action is!

Fourth, all underlying (unconscious) representations are subject to activations, both by external events and by internal (conceptual) processes. The three levels of representation are: unconscious and not recently activated; unconscious but activated (essential the same as the notion of the preconscious); and conscious.

Fifth, activated structures (e.g., schemas) are necessary for the eventual occurrence of effective thought and actions. Only activated structures can be used in conscious constructions. Current models of schema theory and the more sophisticated, but compatible, models of parallel distributed processes are all based on these assumptions.

Sixth, conscious events prime unconscious structures; they provide additional activations to the relevant underlying structures.

The position I endorse had its major start with Marcel whose view of mental structures is concerned with structures and the conditions under which they reach the conscious state.[72] However, in contrast to the view that structures become conscious so that consciousness is simply a different state of a structure,

Marcel sees consciousness as a constructive process in which the phenomenal experience is a novel construction to which two or more activated schemas have contributed. Treisman and Gelade proposed a constructive view of focal attention that is very similar to Marcel's proposition.[73]

A precursor of these views was the theoretical account of automatic activation and conscious processing contributed by Posner and his associates.[74] Conscious processing is described as: "a mechanism of limited capacity which may be directed toward different types of activity."[75] In that sense, this reflects a more traditional position that consciousness is "directed toward" an unconscious structure or process that then becomes "conscious."

The constructive approach to consciousness is also relevant to speculations about the nature of introspective (verbal) reports. Ericsson and Simon have provided an account of the generation of such report, but they are primarily concerned with the relationship between information available in short-term memory (STM) on the one hand and verbalized information on the other.[76] STM seems to operate as a (more respectable?) substitute for consciousness. Ericsson and Simon use "attended to," "heeded," and "stored in STM" as synonymous expressions; recently attended information is kept in STM and is "directly accessible" for producing verbal reports; and the products of automatic processing are not available to STM. The question of what it is that is available in STM (consciousness) is never specifically addressed, but it is implied that that information somehow directly represents cognitive processes. In contrast, I argue that these "available" contents of STM are themselves the product of constructive processes. A theory of introspection needs to specify how "heeding" and "attending" operate and also how such processes determine (construct) specific conscious contents.

We can be conscious only of experiences that are constructed out of activated schemas. We are not conscious of the process of activation or the constituents of the activated schemas. A constructed conscious experience depends on the activated schemas of one or more of the constituent processes and features. I should add here that I find Marcel's argument that necessarily two or more activations are involved in conscious constructions unnecessarily confining.[77] Whereas many conscious constructions involve more than one activated underlying structure there are often instances (e.g., in the insistence of intensive stimuli, whether visual or aural) where single activations issue into consciousness. The advantage of postulating that several activated schemas construct consciousness is that we thereby can achieve the phenomenal unity of conscious experience. Consciousness constructed from more than one activated schema takes advantage of alternate ways of viewing the world and also integrates some optimal amount of the available information. Phenomenal experience is "an attempt to make sense of as much data as possible at the highest or most functionally useful level possible."[78] When a categorical or a value judgment is sought — by an actor's intentions or by an experimenter's instructions — the most functionally useful level of abstraction is a general schema or the relational aspect of a schema. And even then what is constructed as a conscious, phenomenal accompaniment is not the awareness of congruity but the direct apprehension of category membership or valuation. We can go even further and note an early insight of Karl Bühler's that consciousness of a rule is not represented by thinking *of* the rule but it is the thinking a rule or functioning in keeping with the rule.[79]

A relevant interpretation of consciousness was advanced by Roy John. He noted that in consciousness: "information about multiple individual modalities of sensation and perception is combined into a unified multidimensional representation," that is, that "consciousness itself is a representational system."[80] This combination of a number of different, sometimes independent, representations gives rise to the unity of consciousness. No matter how many different pieces of information are presented to us, the conscious experience is practically always a single unified and experientially consistent conscious experience.

As we learn to interpret the significance of a set of cues, "we are aware of that significance instead of and before we are aware of the cues." Although Marcel's argument was specifically intended for the phenomenon of category access without access to instantiation, it applies *pari passu* to a number of judgments, such as evaluation, feeling tone, and general familiarity. Under some conditions of minimal attention to or exposure of instances of verbal or visual categories, there is evidence that people "know" (consciously) to which category a specific event belongs (e.g., furniture, landscape) without being able to identify which particular item (piece of furniture or specific scenes) they had witnessed.[81] Parker has shown that semantic incongruity in a visual display is recognized (peripherally) even before the direct fixation of the incongruous object.[82] It is of course obvious that we are customarily conscious of events and objects in our environ in a constructed fashion; we are aware of the important aspects of the event but hardly ever are aware of all our potential knowledge of the event.[83] Similarly, I would argue it is possible that one can know the value of an event before one is aware of the details of the event that is being judged. A similar disjunction between the awareness of structural and event-specific information has been reported for some time for clinical observations.[84] This general approach to the problem of consciousness of abstract and concrete aspects of an event may also be consistent with those arguments that claim immediate access to complex meanings of events.[85] We are apparently never conscious of all the available evidence that surrounds us but only of a small subset. These observations are illustrations of the proposition that only a limited set of information is available to consciousness and that that limit is restricted to events subjectively important to the individual.

This approach to consciousness suggests highly selective constructions that may be either abstract/general or concrete/specific, depending on what is appropriate to current needs and demands. It is also consistent with phenomenalist arguments that claim immediate access to complex meanings of events. These higher order "meanings" will be readily available whenever the set is to find a relatively abstract construction, a situation frequent in our daily interactions with the world. In summary then, two or more unconscious elements construct a conscious content in response to current needs and demands and as a result of being shaped by the selective limitation and by feedback processes. I should note though that there are frequent cases, particularly in the occurrence of intense single events (loud noises, sensory pains etc) where the access to conscious construction is preempted without preceding constructions as such.

Conscious constructions represent the most general interpretation that is appropriate to the current scene in keeping with both the intentions of the individual and the demands of the environment, and are therefor situationally and culturally determined. In the absence of any specific requirements (internally or externally generated), the current construction will be the most general (or abstract) available. In a problem-solving task, we are conscious of those current mental products that are closest to the task at hand, i.e., the subjectively likely solution to the problem, though not necessarily of course the correct solution.

The notion that the construction out of parts creates the conscious experience is already found in earlier physiological accounts. Henry Head in 1920 noted that "[b]etween the impact of a physical stimulus on the peripheral end organs … and the simplest changes it evokes in consciousness, lie the various phases of physiological activity. The diverse effects … must be sorted and regrouped … until the final products of *integration* … excite those conditions which underlie the … discriminative or … affective aspects of sensation. … a 'primary sensation' is an abstraction."[86] At the other end of the theoretical rainbow and about at the same time Freud saw anxiety as being constructed out of physical sensations and cognitive components. Similarly I argue that consciousness is a constructive process in which the phenomenal experience is a specific construction to which previously activated structures/schemas have contributed. That position rejects the identity assumption, which postulates that conscious states are to be seen as merely another state of a preconscious structure. In contrast, a constructivist position states that most conscious states are constructed out of preconscious structures in response to the requirements of the moment.

We are conscious only of experiences that are constructed out of already activated schemas. Activation does not imply consciousness but activation is necessary before the schema can become conscious. We are customarily conscious of the important aspects of the environs, but never conscious of all the evidence that enters the sensory gateways or of all our potential knowledge of the event. We see crowds and forests but not necessarily specific people or trees until some motive, demand, or need commands such a construction. Attentional processes generate the selection of important and relevant events.

Given that the very confrontation with objects and events may well activate a large number of relevant and often only marginally relevant features and schematic representations, how do only a select few come to consciousness? Why are certain specific ones selected? In the first instance with all the multitude of activated nonconscious elements and features, there is likely to be a large competitive contention for realization into thought and action. As my initial arguments assume, consciousness solves this bottleneck problem by being a limited and serial device (in contrast to the largely unlimited and parallel unconscious). Only some 5–6 organized features or elements are admitted to the final competition and possibly to the conscious state. They are selected and constructed in terms of current needs and demands. In addition, and importantly, they have been shaped by the feedback process of the elements already in a conscious state. I proposed previously that all conscious contents prime related unconscious elements, features, and schemas. These primed activated preconscious elements will then have a privileged position for future selection through the bottleneck process. In this manner the relatedness and relevance of successive conscious contents is assured. Feedback priming produces directed and selective thought.

The feedback function of consciousness

The feedback assumption contrasts with the view that consciousness cannot have any causal effects. Conscious phenomena appear to occur after the event that they register[87] and some authors, particularly of the epiphenomenal persuasion, have insisted that consciousness is causally inert, i.e., has no casual effects on any other mental events or processes. In contrast, the feedback assumption asserts at least one causal utility of conscious events, particularly in their effect on subsequent activations of consciously represented events.[88]

The feedback assumption states that once alternatives, choices, or competing hypotheses have been represented in consciousness they will receive additional activation and thus will be enhanced, i.e., more distinctly and strongly activated for some time. Note that these activations are in addition to the usual flow and spread of activation that takes place during unconscious processing.

Given the capacity limitation of consciousness combined with the intentional selection of conscious states, very few preconscious candidates for actions and thoughts will achieve this additional, consciousness-mediated activation. What structures are most likely to be available for such additional activation? It will be those preconscious structures that have been selected as most responsive to current demands and intentions. Whatever structures are used for a current conscious construction will receive additional activation, and they will have been those selected as most relevant to current concerns. At the same time the phenomenon of spreading activation will activate related, and therefor at least marginally relevant, processes and contents. In contrast, alternatives that were candidates for conscious thought or action but were not selected will be relegated to a relatively lower probability of additional activation and therefore less likely to be accessed on subsequent occasions.

The evidence for this general effect is derived from the vast amount of research showing that the sheer frequency of activation affects subsequent accessibility for thought and action, whether in the area of perceptual priming, recognition memory, preserved amnesic functions, or decision making.[89] The feedback proposal extends such activations to internally generated events and, in particular, to the momentary states of consciousness constructed to satisfy internal and external demands. Thus, just as reading a sentence produces activation of the underlying schemas, so does (conscious) thinking of that sentence or its gist activate these structures. In the former case, what is activated depends on what the world presents to us; in the latter the activation is determined and limited by the conscious construction. Note that in order for the feedback function to make sense, we must assume that the "adaptive" function of construction that selects appropriate, currently relevant mental contents is also operating. In that context one notes, on the one hand, the adaptive function and consequences of feedback whereas, on the other hand, it is quite clear that the feedback sequence and its results is not itself a result of an evolutionary adaptationist event. Rather feedback is another fortuitous consequence of other adaptive and preadaptive processes and functions.

This hypothesis of selective and limited activation of situationally relevant structures requires no homonculus-like function for consciousness in which some independent agency controls, selects, and directs thoughts and actions that have been made available in consciousness. Given an appropriate database, it should be possible to simulate this particular function of consciousness without an appeal to an independent decision-making agency.

The proposal can easily be expanded to account for some of the phenomena of human problem solving. I assume that activation is necessary but not sufficient for conscious construction and that activation depends in part on prior conscious constructions. The search for problem solutions and the search for memorial targets (as in recall) typically have a conscious counterpart, frequently expressed in introspective protocols. What appears in consciousness in these tasks are exactly those points in the course of the search when steps toward the solution have been taken and a choice point has been reached at which the immediate next steps are not obvious. At that point the current state of world is reflected in consciousness. That state reflects the progress toward the goal as well as some of the possible steps that could be taken next. A conscious state is constructed that reflects those aspects of the current search that do (partially and often inadequately) respond to the goal of the search. Consciousness at these points depicts waystations toward solutions and serves to restrict and focus subsequent pathways by selectively activating those that are currently within the conscious construction. Preconscious structures that construct consciousness at the time of impasse, delay, or interruption receive additional activation, as do those still unconscious structures linked with them. The result is a directional flow of activation that would not have happened without the extra boost derived from the conscious state.

Another phenomenon that argues for the re-presentation and re-activation of conscious contents is our ability to "think about" previous conscious contents; we can be aware of our awareness. There is anecdotal as well as experimental evidence that we are sometimes confused between events that "actually" happened and those that we merely imagined, i.e., events that were present in consciousness but not in the surrounds. Clearly the latter must have been stored in a manner similar to the way "actual" events are stored.[90] It has been argued that this awareness of awareness (self-awareness) is in principle indefinitely self-recursive, that is, that we can perceive a lion, be aware that we are perceiving a lion, be conscious of our awareness of perceiving a lion, and so forth.[91] In fact, I have never been able to detect any such extensive recursion in myself, nor has anybody else to my knowledge. We can certainly be aware of somebody (even ourselves) asserting the recursion, but observing it is another matter. The recursiveness in consciousness ends after two or three steps, that is, within the structural limit of conscious organization.

The positive feedback that consciousness provides for activated and constructed mental contents is, of course, not limited to problem-solving situations. It is, for example, evident in the course of self-instructions. In the course of prospective memory we often keep reminding ourselves (consciously) of tasks to be performed, actions to be undertaken. "Thinking about" these future obligations makes it more likely that we will remember to undertake them when the appropriate time arrives. Thus, self-directed comments, such as, "I must remember to write to Mary" or "I shouldn't forget to pick up some bread on the way home," make remembering more and forgetting less likely. Such self-reminding not only keeps the relevant information highly activated but also repeatedly elaborated in different contexts, thus ready to be brought into consciousness when the appropriate situation for execution appears.

Self-directed comments can, of course, be deleterious as well as helpful. The reoccurrence of obsessive thoughts is a pathological example, but everyday "obsessions" are the more usual ones. Our conscious constructions may end up in a loop of recurring thoughts that preempt limited capacity and often prevent more constructive and situationally relevant "thinking." One example is trying to remember a name and getting stuck with an obviously erroneous target that keeps interfering with more fruitful attempts at retrieval. The usual advice to stop thinking about the problem, because it will "come to us" later, appeals to an attempt to let the activation of the "error" return to lower levels before attempting the retrieval once again. The fact that a delay may produce a spontaneous "popping" of the required information speaks to unconscious spreading of activation on the one hand and the apparent restricting effect of awareness on the other. Another example of the deleterious effects of haphazard activation is represented in the likelihood of consciousness being captured by a mundane occurrence. Thus, as we drive home, planning to pick up that loaf of bread, conscious preoccupation with a recent telephone call may capture conscious contents to the exclusion of other, now less activated, candidates for conscious construction, such as the intent to stop at the store. Or, planning to go to the kitchen to turn off the stove, we may be "captured" by a more highly activated and immediate conscious content of a telephone call. The "kitchen-going" intention loses out unless we refresh its activation by reminding ourselves, while on the phone, about the intended task. If we fail to keep that activation strong enough and the plan in mind — our dinner is burned.

The additional function of consciousness as outlined here is generally conservative in that it underlines and reactivates those mental contents that are currently used in conscious constructions and are apparently the immediately most important ones. It also encompasses the observation that under conditions of stress people tend to repeat previously unsuccessful attempts at problem solution. Despite this unadaptive consequence, a reasonable argument can be made that it is frequently useful for the organism to continue to do what apparently is successful and appears to be most appropriate. Finally, the priming functions of consciousness interact in important ways with its construction. If, as I have argued, conscious construction responds to (subjectively) important aspects of the world, then it will be exactly those of course that will be primed and enhanced for future use and access.

However, as a corollary of this mechanism, events that are totally disruptive and inappropriate to the current context should have a quite different function. There is no obvious conscious construction that can be adopted when both the currently dominant action tendencies and their possible alternatives are evidently inadequate. It is at this point that new structures, some of which previously may have been at some relatively weakly activated level, will be called into service. I discuss the emotional (particularly autonomic) consequences of such interruptions and discrepancies in Chapter 6. What I argue here is that in addition to these consequences there are purely mental/cognitive ones. When current activations from the environment, the causes of the disruption, do not readily find an appropriate structure that accommodates to their characteristics, then spreading activation will eventually find some alternative structures that provide some support for the new evidence generated by the world. Novel ways of structuring the world can be found in a variety of situations, some of which are often bizarre or incongruous, whether in science or in science fiction. Such new constructions are also found in dreams, which are not under the control of environmental regularities. The ability to create interruptions, new ways of seeing the world out of joint, seems to be necessary for scientific as well as aesthetic creations. An interesting example is found in the French psychoanalyst

Jacques Lacan's use of the totally unexpected shortening and interruption of his sessions with clients. One participant reports his personal experience with one of Lacan's unexpected short sessions:"The ending of the session, unexpected and unwanted, was like a rude awakening, like being torn out of a dream by a loud alarm. (One patient likened it to *coitus interruptus*)." These short sessions seem to facilitate access to the unconscious and "[t]he combined pressure of the shortness of the sessions and the unpredictability of their stops creates a condition that greatly enhances one's tendencies to free-associate ..."[92]

Unconscious perception

One of the most persistent problems addressed in contemporary experimental psychology concerns the question whether we can register and process information without being conscious that the information had been transmitted to us? I present a discussion of the issue here because it addresses the question how conscious contents — the end result of supra- or subliminal perception — are constructed. I discuss apparently consistent and structured information transmission rather than the more haphazard occurrences of conscious contents which I will introduce in Chapter 5. The notion of unconscious processing is, of course, central to contemporary cognitive psychology. Cognitive psychologists make use of a number of concepts which are closely related to the general notion of the unconscious. For instance, procedural knowledge designates perceptual or motor skills which are performed "automatically" with little or no awareness, and the notion of preattentive processing in the attention literature clearly demands that the stimulus must be analyzed up to a certain level before conscious processing takes place. Moreover, the concept of semantic activation is now pervasive in cognitive science. It is assumed that the processing of the sensory inputs will usually activate representations of features and attributes that constitute concepts and percepts. Semantic activation is often accompanied by subjective experiences, i.e., an awareness of the existence of a stimulus, but the activation of representations in memory *per se* does not necessarily entail subjective awareness on the part of a perceiver.

The problem was brought to the fore in the turmoil about subliminal perception that agitated the psychological and advertising world in the 1960s, when extravagant claims were made that people could be moved to action such as believing propaganda or buying items by just being told to do so by subliminal messages. Subliminal perception research has been one of the major venues in which the relations between the conscious and the unconscious have been investigated.[93]

The modern literature on subliminal perception was initially focused on the question of whether or not such a phenomenon even exists. There were those who argued that there is as yet no convincing evidence that it exists,[94] and those who claimed that the evidence in favor of subliminal perception is overwhelming.[95] The debate has been mainly fueled by conceptual and definitional disagreements over the operationalizing of the concepts of awareness and subliminality in a controlled experimental context.

The major modern experimental discussion started with Eriksen's analysis of unconscious perception in general in the late 1950s and early 1960s. Eriksen's critique resulted in his widely accepted conclusion: "… at present there is no convincing evidence that the human organism can discriminate or differentially respond to external stimuli that are at an intensity level too low to elicit a discriminated verbal report. In other words, a verbal report is as sensitive an indicator of perception as any other response that has been studied."[96] Translating "discriminated verbal report" into a contemporary "being conscious of" the conclusion was that consciousness was a good an indicator of the occurrence of some incoming information as anything else. Thus, the quote implies that there is no (there cannot be) evidence for subliminal discrimination.

Dixon, who was the major defender of subliminal perception, argued for the existence of subliminal perception on the basis of evidence from incidental discrimination: "… the most important feature of subliminal perception is not that people can respond to stimulation below the awareness threshold, but that they can respond to stimulation of which, for one reason or another, they are unaware."[97] In other words, subliminal perception is just an example of unconscious responsiveness to external stimulation, however achieved. Subliminal perception, as defined by Dixon, is present if the subject is not aware of a discrimination even if it is above the discrimination threshold.

An important milestone of the resulting controversy was provided by Bowers, whose central claim has to do with the distinction between the information processed and awareness or consciousness of the processed information.[98] Bowers argued for the need to distinguish perceptions, or rather registrations, and thoughts on the one hand and awareness of these perceptions and thoughts on the other hand. What is implied by this distinction is the notion that perception and cognition are not single either/or events, but complex multi process phenomena taking place over time. Among several implications and consequences of the distinction between perceived information (perceiving) and noticed information (noticing) discussed by Bowers, are the following: Information is registered prior to being (consciously) noticed, and it need not be noticed in order to influence thought and action. What is revealed by introspective reports is what the individual is aware of having perceived rather than what the subject actually processes (perceives or registers). In other words, conscious reports are constructions of accessible information rather than indexes of its mere availability (i.e., the presence of the information as such). Taken together, these propositions make it clear that the criterion of what is perceived is cognitive in a wider sense, while the criterion of what is noticed is a function of specific conscious constructions.

One procedure, which used visual backward masking, has provided a much needed database for evaluating previous subliminal perception research.[99] These studies supported the hypothesis that the processing of word meaning can occur in the absence of conscious perceptual processing. It appeared initially that this finding would make a strong case for the validity of subliminal perception, but since then methodological criticisms have been raised by several researchers, with methodological refinements added to the armamentarium. In particular, Cheesman and Merikle introduced the distinction between objective and subjective thresholds.[100] An objective threshold corresponds to the level of detectability where the discrimination of perceptual information moves above a chance level. In contrast, a subjective threshold corresponds to the level of detectability at which an observer claims just to be able to discriminate perceptual information at better than chance level. The subjective threshold appears to reflect the phenomenological distinction between the unconscious and the conscious better than the objective threshold. At a conceptual level, the earlier investigators adopted a definition of awareness approximated by the objective threshold. But what they actually did at an empirical level was to measure subjective rather than objective detection thresholds. One can then ask the more general question about the difference between the subjective and objective threshold, or — in Bowers' terms — the difference between noticing and perceiving an event.

There is some evidence that there may not be much difference between the two thresholds. Nakamura studied masked perception of simple letters.[101] For the objective threshold subjects were asked to indicate which of five letters had been presented (and to guess if unsure). For the subjective threshold they were asked whether they had seen nothing, any part of a letter, or a fairly complete letter. If the subjective threshold is defined as seeing anything at all, the objective threshold seems to occur at about the same exposure level as the subjective threshold. If one asks for the conscious perception of a whole letter then the subjective threshold apparently occurs at a greater exposure time than the objective one. In other words the distinction between the two thresholds may depend on the criteria used for either or both. If the processing of information is restricted to perceptual features and semantic processing is inhibited, people will show the same unconscious effect of prior processing in the absence of being able to (consciously) remember the presented material.[102]

Unconscious representations can produce different conscious constructions
The distinction between subjective and objective judgments and similar differentiations illustrates that the same underlying representations may produce different conscious constructions. The fact that people develop representations not only of their perceptions, thoughts, and actions but also about these products is by now well established. One of the important distinctions that needs to be kept in mind in studying consciousness is that between the underlying structures (and schemas) that construct thought and actions on the one hand, and on the other hand the cognitive structures which are glosses on, which describe and (sometimes) access the determining structures. These secondary structures are particularly evident with respect to action systems, which often remain permanently inaccessible to conscious construction. What is represented in consciousness, and available for introspective reports, often is not a reflection of the operating processes and structures at all.

A detailed discussion of the relation between putative cognitive processes and conscious reports has been presented by Nisbett and Wilson. In areas as diverse as attribution studies, perception, problem solving, choice, prediction, and emotional reactions, they present convincing evidence of a lack of correlation between what people report to have experienced and what (objectively) took place. Only when conditions are salient and are themselves plausible causes of the actions they produce are these reports likely to be accurate. Nisbett and Wilson concluded that experiential reports "are based on a priori, implicit causal theories, or judgments about … a plausible cause of a given response."[103] These implicit theories are frequently the folk theories about thought and action that inform the members of a culture about plausible (socially agreed on) causes.

Whenever a conscious content is constructed that seeks to recover an intrapsychic series of events that occurred some time in the past, it should be obvious that such constructions will be influenced by current as well as past activations. As a result, introspective reports will very often reflect not what "actually" happened, but rather what is the most reasonable construction at the moment of introspection.

The major sources of calling for a particular construction are current tasks and contexts, intentions, and needs. Just as current perceptions are, within schema theory, seen as the result of both external evidence and internal processes (bottom up and top down), so is consciousness in general determined by activated higher-order structures as well as by the evidence from the environment. Structures that represent intentions and interpretations of situational requirements are activated primarily "top down;" they depend on prior evaluations, on activations of situational identifications and interpretations, and on current needs and goals. They need not — like many schemas — receive activation from the physical evidence of our surroundings. In the normal course of events, the more abstract and general structures define what we are doing, what we want to do, and need to do. When task and intention are narrowed down to particulars, less general and more specific schemas determine conscious constructions.

Consider the Nakamura experiment discussed above. Subjects were given the five letters from which the exposed stimulus had been chosen and asked to select (guess) which of the five letters had been exposed, or they were asked to report whether they had seen nothing, part of a letter, or a full letter. Subjects were no better at the "automatic" choice than in conscious discrimination. If, however, subliminal perception is more strictly defined, i.e., as a report of having seen the whole letter, conscious perception of a whole letter is functionally not as good as the choice of the correct letter. The data show that the same underlying presentation (i.e., the activation of the relevant letter representation) can give rise to two different, but functionally equivalent, overt (conscious?) events. Both the choice of a letter and "seeing" a letter or part of it are constructions arising from the same representation. Which construction occurs depends on the demands of the task.

An interesting illustration of a single underlying process being represented in at least two different ways in consciousness can be found in signal detection analyses of recognition memory. Experimental subjects may be required either to make a yes/no judgment on old and new events (usually words) independently, or they might make a forced choice decision among two or three alternatives presented simultaneously. In the former case, the conscious representation is one of making decisions with false alarms being presumably experienced as previously seen or heard events. In the forced choice case, the task is experienced as one of choice and by the nature of the task there are no false alarms as such. However, signal detection theory has shown that the two different methods produce the identical index of discriminability.[104] The two tests yield the same result despite different conscious representations.

Relatively simple perceptual structures, such as reversible and ambiguous figures, also exhibit alternative conscious representations. A single stimulus event forms the basis of different conscious representations, but in consciousness all but one of the alternatives are excluded. The phenomenon also demonstrates the serial nature of conscious representations.

The limitation of conscious experience

The limitation of consciousness to some few items seems well justified by the facilitation of decision making and having appropriate actions readily available. Fascination with the phenomenon goes back at least 300 years. One of the earliest references to the limitation of human attention was made by Charles Bonnet (1720–1793). Antoine Louis Claude Destutt de Tracy (1754–1836) elaborated on the notion that only six "objects" can be apprehended by the mind at any one time. Hamilton introduced the notion into the modem era and noted that it applied to both single objects and groupings of objects.[105] By 1890 William James had firmly established the limited capacity concept as a cornerstone of our knowledge about consciousness/attention, and G. A. Miller made it a central thesis of modern approaches to human information processing.[106] One of the outcomes of the preoccupation was the definition and naming of the process of the rapid and accurate appreciation of small (less than 6) collections of objects as "subitizing."[107]

George Miller had noted the restriction of accurate perception to some few items in psychophysical experiments, but that restriction applies — as one would expect — to everyday activities as well. Given arrays of choices from which to buy or select people are more likely to select/buy from sets of 6 items than from sets of 30.[108] I assume that larger numbers of choices make it difficult to compare alternatives and the set that is being examined may in fact change from instant to instant

The limited capacity of consciousness should be an excellent candidate as a pervasive characteristic of human beings. Behavior geneticists who are eager to ascribe evolutionary and genetic origins to a variety of human characteristics and differences might well focus on limited conscious capacity, which is found across groups, societies, races, and even ages. As Dempster noted in an extensive review of the available data: "there is little or no evidence of either individual or developmental differences in capacity." He defines capacity as "attentional capacity" or as the limited amount of attention that is available "for activating internal units stored in long-term memory."[109] I assume in the first place that the limited-capacity characteristic of consciousness serves to reduce further the "blooming confusion" that the physical world potentially presents to the organism. Just as sensory end organs and central transducers radically reduce and categorize the world of physical stimuli to the functional stimuli that are in fact registered, so does the conscious process further reduce the available information to a small and manageable subset. I assume, somewhat circularly, that the limitation of conscious capacity defines what is in fact cognitively manageable. Whereas we do not know why the reduction is of the magnitude that we observe, it is reasonable to assume that some reduction is necessary. Just consider a need for pairwise comparisons (in a choice situation) among n chunks in consciousness; clearly the number n must be limited if the organism is to make a choice within some reasonable time span.

There are occasions and stimuli that demand conscious capacity and construction almost automatically. Among these are intense stimuli and internal physiological events such as autonomic nervous system activity. Whenever such events claim and preoccupy some part of the limited-capacity system, other cognitive functions will suffer, i.e., they will be displaced from conscious processing and problem-solving activities will be impaired. Particularly in the case of the interruption or failure of ongoing conscious (and particularly unconscious) intercourse with the world, signals from both the external and the internal world will require conscious representation.

The question arises whether we are really "conscious" of five or six discrete events. The arguments for a constructive view of consciousness seem to counsel against such a view. If we consider consciousness as an integrated construction of the available evidence — a construction that seems to be phenomenally "whole" — then it is probably more likely that the limitation to a certain number of items or objects or events or chunks refers to the limitation of these elements within the constructed holistic conscious experience. I would argue therefore that whatever schema guides the conscious experience it is necessarily restricted to a certain number of features or relations. Cognitive "chunks " — organized clusters of knowledge — can operate as units of such constructed experience, just as the experience itself acts as a constructed holistic chunk. For example, as I look out of my window I am aware of the presence of trees and roads and people — individual organized schemas. I may switch my attention

— reconstruct my conscious experience — to focus on one of these events and note that some of the people are on bicycles, others walk, some are male, some female. Switching attention again I see a friend and note that he is limping, carrying a briefcase, and talking with a person walking next to him. In each case a new experiential whole enters the conscious state and it itself consists of new and different organized chunks.

In arguing that the limited capacity of consciousness is represented by the number of events that can be organized within a single constructed conscious experience, I respond to the intuitively appealing notion that we are both aware of some unitary "scene" and have available within it a limited number of constituent chunks. I have discussed in Chapter 1 the manner in which these momentary conscious states construct the phenomenal continuity and flow of consciousness.

The construction of individual chunks is consistent with the cognitive mechanisms embodied in the distinction between integrative and elaborative processing.[110] Integration refers to the process whereby the elements of a structure become more strongly related to each other, the structure itself develops its own unique constituents, and relations among the elements of a cognitive structure (a schema) become stable. This process produces organized chunks of knowledge that act as single units, are stored and retrieved as units, and may themselves become elements or features of a larger cognitive structure. Elaboration on the other hand refers to the establishment of relationships among structures, the kind of network that is basic to the notion of structural meaning. The relations of a unit of knowledge to other such units determines its meaning and its function in memorial storage and retrieval. Integration and elaboration have a dialectic relationship. The integration of a particular set of elements may be viewed as the elaboration of one of its constituent members, and conversely elaboration of a particular event involves the integration of the events that are related to the target event.

I now move on to more detailed topics, but first take a quick look at some other speculations about consciousness.

Chapter 4

Nihil tam absurde… demystifying consciousness

This chapter surveys a selected subset of views on consciousness. My review will be outspoken and at times jaundiced. I start with four positions that have generally been taken toward conscious phenomena: epiphenomenal, directive, intentional, and constructivist.

Consciousness as epiphenomenon. This position assumes that some mental processes and contents are consciously accessible. But their conscious status is not generally relevant to ongoing mental processes and — in particular — they do not interact with such processes. Nothing different would happen if there were no conscious contents and processes. This position has been found attractive by psychologists and cognitive scientists of varying persuasions. It was, of course, one of the central behaviorist contentions, but epiphenomenalism is alive today, e.g., among some computationally oriented cognitive scientists. One of the best metaphors that illustrates the position is the suggestion that "consciousness may be like the heat or the hum or the smell of the computer."[111] Most epiphenomenalists are examples of the attitude typified by one of their numbers — Jackendoff who, being enchanted with a computational view of mind, sees consciousness as a reflection of mental computations, concluding that "consciousness is not good for anything."[112] Patricia Churchland, who in the 1980s characterized consciousness' irrelevance as being "like the sound that rain makes" has adapted her position to a more positive attitude. And then there is Thagard, who drew the peculiar conclusion that whereas consciousness has no function for cognitive (real?) science, it may have some uses for social and educational psychology. But then how does the mind know when it should be in one mode or the other? For more aspects of epiphenomenalism, see Flanagan who has usefully discussed and implicitly dismissed it.[113]

Consciousness as directive or executive. The assumption is that the conscious status of some mental contents has a special importance, and may have some effects — usually by directing or organizing mental contents. Conscious contents make possible the manipulation of underlying structures. Psychoanalysis is an example of this position, though of course it also endows unconscious processes with directive properties. The most popular current version is that of consciousness as a central executive. The generalized form from a computational position is that consciousness may be a property of certain classes of automata, and that it has directive and selective functions.[114] Baars (see below) sometimes comes close to the "executive" position.

Consciousness and intentionality. The third general position on consciousness sees subjective experience as a necessary condition for intentionality. Intentionality may be briefly and inadequately defined as the *aboutness* of mental states, i.e., that mental states have intrinsic semantic contents. Its relation to consciousness arises out of the assertion that the ability to have subjective experiences is necessary for "understanding," for imbuing mental acts with semantic contents.[115] This position is particularly associated with John Searle,[116] but has other advocates, such as Thomas Nagel and Donald Griffin.[117] Griffin, in particular, illustrates the nature of this enterprise when he infers intentional states from the observed complex behavior of lower animals, and then takes the second speculative leap of inferring subjective consciousness from the inferred intentionality. Van Gulick has shown that the conjunction of intentionality and consciousness is not as clear as it seems to its defenders,[118] and several of Griffin's fascinating demonstrations suggest that nonintentional machines could produce similar actions. One also needs to consider the possibility that in some few cases the subjective experience accompanying intentional acts may be no more than a conscious gloss on the action and not a necessary condition for it.

Consciousness as a constructed device. The constructivist position states that conscious contents are constructed from unconscious ones; they may be identical with them but frequently (usually) are not. It is also associated with many psychological positions that inquire as to the useful or adaptive functions of consciousness. Just as for the executive position, the constructivist view sees consciousness as a serial device interacting with the parallel architecture of the mental system. It derives the functions of constructed consciousness from psychological rather than computational considerations and lessens, if not eliminates, the homunculus functions of consciousness. In addition, the conscious representation has several more or less automatic effects that interact with decision processes, memory functions, etc.

Finally there are a variety of philosophical positions that do not easily fall into any of the categories I discussed above. I will discuss some of the more surprising (and sometimes outrageous) ones. The philosophy of mind and consciousness, fairly recently awakened from a place-holding slumber, abounds with conjectures and speculations. Just the sheer number and variety of labels for different and contradictory positions in philosophy are enough to deter one from trying to summarize "contemporary" philosophy. Here is a sample: Eliminative materialism, analytic functionalism, analytic behaviorism, homuncular functionalism, direct realism, commonsense relationism, and many more. It might be useful if philosophers could agree on some basic propositions (even testable ones?) so that the rest of us could derive some benefit from their labors. Or maybe we should just charitably accept current philosophy if in fact the twentieth century is "the silliest of all the centuries, philosophically speaking."[119]

I continue with a view of current philosophical and psychological and evolutionary thought. More extended discussions of these and related positions are discussed in the later section on interpretations of mind.

Nihil tam absurde...[120] philosophies of consciousness

I believe that the search for an understanding of consciousness has been seriously impaired by the speculative floods that philosophers started dispensing some 20 years ago. I have great respect for many strains of philosophy and particularly for many philosophers of science, but philosophies of the mind have gone over the top — with little regard for evidence or for the functions of consciousness. Their activities demonstrate an old story:

A new university was being planned. The chairs of all the new department are called in to describe their material needs. Physics needs an accelerator and a few hundred million worth of buildings and equipment, chemistry and biology do not lag far behind, but soon the demands become smaller and smaller. Eventually the mathematician comes in and announces that hers will be a theoretical department so all they really need is offices, pads of yellow paper, pencils, and waste paper baskets. The last supplicant is the philosopher who admits to having overheard the previous interview and requests the same constellation, except "we will not need the waste paper baskets."

The difficulty with philosophy is not only with the content of what many of its practitioners say but with their acceptance of a method that is designed to generate insight as well as nonsense, discoveries as well as banalities. It is a method explicitly or implicitly based on a belief in the rationality and creativity of human thought. Any deliberation of a minimally prepared mind on any topic, as long as that deliberation is earnest and extended, is permitted and no evidence need to be adduced as to the results of these deliberations. When philosophers criticize one another they typically attack the content of the contribution but rarely the method.

Some specific examples[121]

There is a subset of philosophers that holds a relatively mystical position on consciousness. For them consciousness may be in principle unanalyzable and forever opaque to any kind of scientific analysis or understanding. Take for example McGinn who proposes an unknowability position, that we will never understand consciousness, and also, without much attempt at justification, asserts that in the absence of consciousness mind would "evaporate into thin air."[122] For an equivalent position on mind (consciousness?) see my discussion of Nagel below.

Another position simply denies the reality of human experience. Paul Churchland has stayed faithful to his original scientific position that we can (and must) overcome our submission to the folk psychology (*sic)* of qualia by acting and thinking more directly in terms of neurological function, so that a "pain" will become something like the "activation of neurons 230a and 782x."[123] He argues for bypassing "folk psychology" and having direct access to (direct inspection of) our neurophysiology, i.e., we will eventually "see" a wavelength rather then a color. Apart from the patent nonsense of a position which denies human passion and aesthetics, which state of neurophysiological knowledge — 1900, 2000, or 3000 — are we supposed to "experience", to live by? Churchland's eliminative materialism jumps (frolicks?) from folk psychology to neurophysiology, dismissing psychology on the way. He joins other philosophers who either explicity or implicitly equate folk psychology with the discipline of psychology, in the process psychological attempts to account for memory, learning, dreams, etc. are often baldly dismissed. But eliminative materialism, like so many philosophical positions, is an assertion of faith — and therefor makes no testable assertions, summarizes no data, and cannot be proved wrong.

Block comes close to a quasi-mystical position when he tries to distinguish conscious from unconscious awareness.[124] He distinguishes p-(phenomenal) and a-(access) consciousness — the latter is not phenomenal, it is "poised" and it is representational, it sounds much like preconsciousness, so why use a new and very confusing concept? The tendency to take generally usable common language terms like "conscious" and turn them around for purposes of an intellectual pirouette may be catching. Elster, for example, has pursued — as others have done — the notion of unconscious emotions.[125]

In the face of much philosophical obscurantism Güzeldere has provided an even handed and comprehensible summary of the varieties of philosophical speculations. There are other philosophers who have been willing to consider empirical questions and philosophical positions, among them Robert Van Gulick, Virginia Hardcastle, and Patricia Kitcher.

Consider for example Hardcastle's position: Using psychological research extensively, she postulates three memory systems: Skill memories, perceptual (implicit) memory, and structural (semantic) memory. It is the latter that produces explicit memory and is responsible for consciousness. This fails to give the full flavor of a complex systematic account that draws heavily on neurophysiology, but does not deal with problems of functional utility and evolution.[126]

Psychological positions

The most extensive and ambitious psychological theory of consciousness is Baars', and it is not easily summarized.[127] It covers most of the conscious activities of human, though it discusses only cursorily such things as dreams, is fuzzy on attention, and seems to put the weight of mental function on conscious, rather than unconscious, activities. As far as the problem of subjective consciousness is concerned, Baars elevates the "self" to the status of observer of mental acitivity. It is not at all clear how the self, observing the mind at work, itself becomes in some sense "conscious." In general the theory posits a large number of unconscious structures ("contexts") that compete for conscious access and whose products are then broadcast to the entire global workspace. However, it is a theory concerned with function rather than with philosophical speculations and therefore is to be applauded.

I have discussed Michael Posner's important contributions to the early exploratiomns of consciousness within a functional psychological context in Chapters 1 and 2. He has also presented significant explorations of attention and the relations between attention and consciousness which I discuss in Chapter 5.

Shallice, whose contribution I also mentioned briefly in Chapter 1, reviewed the state of art as of a decade ago.[128] His earlier model is clearly a relative of my own presentation. It suggests that only one action system (schema?) is maximally activated, and therefore conscious, at any one time.[129] Consciousness plays the important role of selecting such an action system and in its emphasis on limited actions and selection the model is obviously a forerunner of my own thoughts.

Several other psychological positions are discussed in the next section.

Some evolutionary positions

For reasons that I have spelled out above I will not discuss neurobiological positions at length. There are a number of informed discussions of possible evolutionary scenarios of consciousness from a neurobiological point of view.[130] However these discussions are generally vague about the adaptive functions of consciousness. Natural selection operates on the functioning organism. We need to know first in detail what it is that consciousness does for the organism before it is useful to discuss its neurobiology. Detailed discussions of the neurological evolution at the present time puts the cart before the horse.

There are relatively few psychologists who have extensively concerned themselves with the evolution of consciousness. William James adopted the evolutionary argument that no biological structures/phenomena exist that have not been generated by the process of natural selection, and he then extends this logically and naturally to feelings/qualia, but further implies that therefor these feelings must be adaptive. And since feelings (and *per extenso qualia*) are products of evolutionary processes they must have effects in the material world. James also noted that consciousness was an invention of nature in order to deal with the overpowering complexity of the underlying physiological processes.[131]

James' argument about feelings as products of evolution was extended by Cairns-Smith who argued that since qualia are the products of natural selection which works only on the material worlds, qualia therefor belong to the material world. His extensive discussion also suggests that one of the functional uses of consciousness is that it provides us with a model of the external world.[132]

One of the more ambitious excursions into the evoluion of consciousness and thought has been Nicholas Humphrey's.[133] He starts off with postulating an animal that is highly intelligent and motivated but has "no picture of what this brain-computer is doing or how it works. The animal is in effect an unconscious Cartesian automaton."[134] He then assumes that a new sense organ, an "inner eye" evolves whose field of view is the brain itself. This new organ is produced by natural selection and tells the subject as much about her brain function as she is likely to understand. Thus brain states are seen as conscious states of mind. Humphrey sees consciousness as a surface feature which has been added to the functioning organism as a self-reflective loop. He argues that consciousness — as a product of evolution — should help the conscious individual to survive and reproduce, and concludes that the information provided by consciousness must be useful for survival and reproduction. I find this reasoning somewhat circular in that it assumes what is deduced. But the attempt is important since it again is thrust in the direction of finding what functions consciousness may perform — and therefor have been selected.

MacPhail has advocated an essentially epiphenomenalist position, seeing no particular functions for consciousness but asserting that the development of a powerful "self" from infancy on generates consciousness as a byproduct.[135] I stress again that self is just another schema, but one built up longer than any others, more complex and elaborate, and it is the invocation of the self schema what we mean when we have self experiences.

There is no particular reasons why the "self" needs to be elevated to a regnant position in the human mind — all the relevant evidence suggests that it works like a well established assembly of observations, perceptions and intentions about one's own person — physically and psychologically. It is probably best seen as another example of need to see humans as some unique and exalted product of evolution, spirit, etc. I like a quote from the Hindu sage Shankaracharya that "The 'I' is an illusion, but that illusion needs to be experienced, and it is only by experiencing it that it can be known as illusion."[136]

In September 2000 a debate was held in London in which four prominent scientists addressed the question: Can evolutionary theory explain the presence of consciousness? The announcement said: "Consciousness seems central to human life. But neural processing in the brain does not seem to require it. So, why are human beings conscious? According to evolutionary theory, consciousness must be an adaptation that enhances reproductive fitness. But, if brains or computers could function just as well without it, why and how did consciousness appear? And, if consciousness is not an adaptation, what consequences are there for evolutionary theory? In tonight's debate, four scientists who have all worked on consciousness, but arrived at very different conclusions, discuss these issues."

The speakers and their topics were:

Euan Macphail: The evolution of language is the key to the evolution of consciousness.

Stevan Harnad: Consciousness cannot be functional, it can just be.

Jeffrey Gray: Evolutionary theory must be able to explain the existence of consciousness (but I haven't the faintest idea how).

Max Velmans: Evolutionary theory can account for the forms of consciousness but not its existence.

This is just one example how perfectly reasonable people can be led astray when delving into something which *a priori* they consider to be mysterious. For example what can the fact that computers are not conscious have possibly to do with consciousness in humans. Computers cannot be pregnant either but that is not considered relevant to problems of human pregnancies. And how brains incorporate some direct representation of consciousness is, at the present time, at least not unknown — certainly it cannot be prejudged.

The titles give away the speakers various position: Macphail makes the *a priori* decision that animals without language cannot be conscious, Harnad presents the usual epiphenomenal cop out, Gray is willing to be reasonable, and Velmans is the representative of mysticism.

Philosophy and psychology of mind

Philosophers and others are often fascinated by the puzzle of the subjective "mind," the "irreducibly subjective character of conscious mental processes."[137] It is undoubtedly the case that contents are interpretatively subjective (i.e., that their meaning is a function of the conscious person's unique semantics), and that the experience is restricted to the subject. However, both common experience and scientific history tell us that just because direct experience is not available to us, this does not mean that we cannot profitably use indirect methods, both simple and complex, to make sense of those hidden events. In the absence of direct access, sophisticated theory is available here as it has been in other areas. There is nothing magical about consciousness that might prevent us from developing a useful and predictive theory about it.

The basic problem that philosophers have created was starkly presented by Descartes and his assertion of the infallibility of the conscious world — what we can consciously experience is not to be doubted. The external, physical world, on the other hand, was not definitively ascertainable from within the Cartesian theatre.[138] That position was undermined by the various positivists and their precursors who made the verification of scientific assertions a cornerstone of their position. Verificationism led to the insistence on a shared protocol language about public events. Such an elevation of public consensus about the physical world questioned the apparent dominant position of the inner theatre and gave valuable support to the behaviorism of the early 20th century. The behaviorists, for their own reason and history, ruled the inner world out of court. J.B. Watson, arguably a man of limited vision and talent, simply declared consciousness of no scientific value or interest. More sophisticated behaviorists, such as B.F. Skinner — the major creative mind of the movement — easily admitted the existence of private events but because of the lack of verifiability and the absence of specific links to external events Skinner denied them any causal significance, a position shared by many philosophers and psychologists for often different reasons. On the other hand, Skinner would not have any truck with mentalism,[139] and some philosophers seem puzzled that Skinner admitted the inner events but declined to consider them mental.[140] Once again we are faced with the sometime identification of consciousness with mind, though we rarely encounter an unequivocal definition of the latter.

There are two major problems confronting an attempt to delimit a philosophy of mind. First, some philosophers are not at all sure that it would be possible to arrive at any understanding of mind, whatever it is. And second, there is no agreement whether "mind" refers to the contents of consciousness or whether something else or more is implied.

Thomas Nagel is an excellent example of a philosopher who, though implicitly claiming otherwise, denies the possibility of understanding the mind, without quite telling us what this "mind" might be. It is described as a "general feature of the world" like matter that cannot be understood by any physical reduction and which also is beyond any evolutionary explanation. Nagel assures us that "something else" must be going on, and he is sure that whatever it may be, it is taking us to a "truer and more detached" understanding of the world.[141] Whereas I do not wish to advertise any great advance in contemporary psychology, it is difficult to follow someone who on the one hand refuses to examine current psychological knowledge and on the other hand insists that "the methods needed to understand ourselves do not yet exist" (p. 10). Nagel contends that "the world may be inconceivable to *our* minds." Humans are by no means omniscient, but one cannot truly claim to know or to prejudge what knowledge is or is not attainable. There surely are aspects of the world that are currently inconceivable, and others that were so centuries ago, but many of the latter are not now and the former may not be in the future.

There seems to be no public agreement as to the referent for the ubiquitous term "mind," and dictionaries are not particularly helpful. For example, Webster's is quite catholic in admitting "the complex of elements in an individual that feels, perceives, thinks, wills, and esp. reasons" AND "the conscious mental events and capabilities in an organism" AND "the organized conscious and unconscious adaptive mental activity of an organism." Philosophers rarely tell us which of these minds they have in mind. One wonders how obscure these deliberations must appear to a French or German reader who has no exact equivalent for our "mind" and must rely on *esprit, Sinn, Seele, Geist,* or *Psyche.* Apart from the public display of disunity, it is likely that most philosophers would agree to a use of "mind" as a quasi-theoretical entity that is causally involved in mental events, including consciousness. I will return to the conflict between seeing "mind" as representing the contents (and sometimes functions) of consciousness compared with using "mind" as a summary term for the various mechanisms that we assign to conscious and unconscious processes.

Having happily accepted one or another form of Cartesian dualism for nearly 300 years, Anglophone philosophy briefly partook of behaviorist escapades in the first half of the 20th century while wrestling with the purified attitudes of logical positivism. Things changed radically around 1960 with the advent of the currently favored way of dealing with the mind — functionalism.[142] At its simplest, philosophical functionalism depends on sensory inputs and observable behaviors linked by a set of causal relations to describe (in various ways) the"how" of consciousness and mind.

Partly in reaction against the identity theory of mind and brain,[143] philosophical functionalism was part of the general change in the cognitive and social sciences that took place in the late 1950s and early 1960s. Lycan, in defending a strong version of functionalism as "honest-to-goodness natural teleology," is interested in the various components as they serve (weakly teleologically) the supervening current operation or function of a system.[144] He invokes a hierarchical system for all complex phenomena with any level of the hierarchy being unpacked into many lower levels of lesser complexity, thus avoiding the problem of a simple homuncular regression.[145] The general concern — here and elsewhere — is with mechanisms; how does the system/mind/organism manage relations between inputs and outputs, and how does it achieve a particular state? Van Gulick similarly uses functionalism to define psychological (conscious) states within a network of perceptual conditions and organism behaviors. He concludes that such a functional approach permits us to think about content in a naturalistic way and to discern continuities that fit the facts about content.[146] I stress this approach because it focuses on the distinction between philosophical and psychological functionalism. Approaching that difference, Sober made a distinction between the dominant Machine Functionalism and Teleological Functionalism. In contrast to the "how" questions of Machine Functionalism, the Teleological variety asks also what the functions of particular system/organs/processes are.[147] It is this sense of functionalism which asks the kind of questions that psychologists prefer, and which treat various positions as ostensibly fallible theories about consciousness (or the mind). I should add that I do not believe that this kind of psychological functionalism falls under the rubric of functional analyses and their problems.[148] Rather than say, for example, that "consciousness has the function of making unconscious material available for further processing," I prefer to approach a sense of function as in "How does consciousness function (operate) in and contribute to an information processing system?"

Many of the philosophers' concerns center on the status of common sense, everyday folk psychology (FP). There appears to be some underlying notion that FP characterizes the psychology that most psychologists do. When philosophers reject FP they reject it frequently on grounds similar to those used by psychologists. On the other hand, the employment by psychologists of such theoretical notions as schemas, (unconscious) organizations and strategies, mental and/or neural activation, and so forth, as well as the absence in most current psychological theories of such beloved folk-theoretical terms as belief, attitude, and will, clearly differentiate FP and psychological psychology. One can even argue that a consequential theory of cognitive processes does not involve intentionality (however defined) but rather that intentional states are one of the phenomena to be explicated and understood by a psychological theory. When rejecting FP, philosophers rarely use an appropriate and convenient psychological theory to contrast with it, but prefer to strike out on their own. For example, Paul Churchland demonstrated that the (much maligned) FP is a theory about the mind and then claimed to show how, as a theory, it is false. However, as I have implied earlier, Churchland's eliminative materialism[149] — an equally fallible theory seems even less plausible than folk psychology and is unlikely to replace it.

Two classes of opinion on mind and consciousness deviate from the mainstream positions outlined here. One group — the deniers — asserts the causal inertness or functional irrelevance of consciousness, the other — the innovators — invokes a novel view of the central nervous system in order to account for conscious phenomena.

The major players in the denial groups are those who cannot conceive any possible functional significance of consciousness. They at least discuss (and dismiss) the possibility that consciousness has some important mental functions, in contrast to those who do not even consider such functionality. An interesting position is held by Gregory who denies consciousness any functional significance because it occurs *after* the event to which consciousness is relevant.[150]

Among the innovators, several recent attempts have made relatively little contact with either philosophy or with phenomenal consciousness directly. The two most visible have been Penrose's and Edelman's accounts.[151] Penrose, who ambitiously wishes to involve some future quantum theory with a causal account of consciousness, is the most creative and challenging of the various contemplators of consciousness. However, I believe his argument that brains and minds are not computers is overwrought and tilts at windmills that have currently only a few hot winds at their service; most of us know that minds are not digital computers, and Penrose's positive arguments about some future quantum-theoretical account is generally devoid of current evidence and ignores psychological insights and evidence about differences between conscious and unconscious processes. Edelman actually presents more an innovative theory of cognition and memory than a theory of consciousness. The latter is brought in as a result of perceptual categorization and its relation to memory — a sort of feedback or reentrant mechanism that "creates" consciousness. Edelman is persuasive and makes important arguments, but he seems not quite clear how a necessary consciousness fits into his ambitious and complex machinery of mind.

I have previously noted the point of view that mind and consciousness are coextensive, I now wish to consider another position that sees mind as the sum total of mechanisms that we ascribe to people (or even to nonhuman animals) in order to make their behavior understandable and coherent. Such a position sees mind and consciousness as independent, though related, concepts; it is implicitly present in many psychological discussions of mind and has been at times explicitly defined. For example, some 50 years ago, Karl Deutsch suggested that "*Mind* might be provisionally defined as any self-sustaining physical process which includes the seven operations of abstracting, communicating, storing, subdividing, recalling, recombining and reapplying items of information."[152] Such an approach to mind as a collection of mechanisms is also implied by some philosophers, even though they are preoccupied with the mental functions of consciousness. For example, Searle, who sometimes confuses consciousness and mind, notes that "most of the mental phenomena in [a] person's existence are not present to consciousness" and "most of our mental life at any given point is unconscious."[153] He then, however, maintains that our access to unconscious mental states is derived solely from conscious mental states. Not only does such a view signal a return to an initial *tabula rasa* that only becomes populated by the individual's experiences, but it also denies any kind of acquisition of skills or knowledge without conscious participation or any kind of preexperientially given structures.

For example, we (and children of 5 and younger) speak our language grammatically correct without having any idea, "being conscious", of the rules that govern such grammaticality. I used to ask my undergraduate students which of two sentences: "The red beautiful rose" or "the beautiful red rose" sounded RIGHT and why, whereupon they practically unanimously picked the second one, and generated many and sometimes wondrous explanations without any noticeable agreement. The unconscious is continuously accessed, and mostly without any conscious accompaniment. Philosophers frequently find these examples challenging and often full of mystery. But that is only the case if one believes in the ubiquity and necessity of consciousness to make a mind. To repeat, it is the unconscious where the action is.

And finally, if mind is the repository of perceptual, cognitive, behavioral mechanisms then it can also be argued to be the function that is performed by the brain (see also below). If "mind is what the brain does," then similar relations can be seen in the form and function of other human organs, such as livers and kidneys. A related sentiment is echoed in Lycan's statement that "the mystery of the mental is no more a mystery than the heart, the kidney, the carburetor or the pocket calculator."[154]

Yes, Virginia, there is a brain: The mind–body distinction[155]

There is, strictly speaking, no mind–body *problem*; dealing with so-called minds is not incompatible with a modern materialism. Mind is what the brain does; just as energy conservation is what a liver does. There are specific functions associated with large operational units such as organs, organisms, and machines, and these functions (and their associated concepts) cannot without loss of meaning be reduced to the constituent processes of the larger units. The speed of a car, the conserving function of the liver, and the notion of a noun phrase are not reducible to internal-combustion engines, liver cells, or neurons. Emergence is a label that has often been applied to these new properties of larger assemblies. Similarly, Searle notes that consciousness is an emergent feature of neurons just as solidity and liquidity are emergent features of molecules, and he also argues that consciousness might be distributed over large portions of the brain.[156] Just as philosophers have advanced a multitude of interpretations of mind and consciousness, so have neurophysiologists and neuropsychologists proposed many different suggestions for the physical location or realization of consciousness. Kinsbourne has summarized some of the various localizations that have been proposed.[157] These range from Descartes' pineal gland to Baars specialized work space[158] and there are many others in between. Following an extensive review of conscious functions and possible structures, Kinsbourne concludes that consciousness is a function of complex brains, in keeping with Sherrington's assertion that there is no microscopical, physical or chemical clue to consciousness, only greater complexity.[159] This conclusion is consistent with the psychological arguments about the need for some such function as consciousness when information processing brains become large and very complex. The argument about consciousness as an emergent function of brains needs also to be placed in the context of reductionist arguments. Most current commentators are materialists and as materialists they subscribe to the first part of what Weinberg has called *grand reductionism,* i.e., "the view that all of nature is the way it is … because of simple universal laws, to which in some sense all other scientific laws may in some sense be reduced."[160] The claim of reduction contained in the second half does not follow, and it actually only refers to a subset of materialist dogma, i.e., physicalism. In any case, complex emergent functions need their own laws and principles which cannot without loss of meaning be reduced to the "universal laws."[161]

Given the variety of suppositions about the neural basis of consciousness that is available, I do not wish to discuss their contentions nor particularly advocate one or the other. I do note however that the notion that consciousness is a function of complex brains and not especially localized is consistent with my basic hypothesis. If consciousness is no more or less than the selection of important currently relevant perceptions, conception or reactions to internal and external events, then its particular material basis will be associated with those preconscious mechanisms and actions that have been selected. As a consequence there will be no single physiological counterpart associated with consciousness, but rather it will vary with the particular location of the currently activated representations.

Finally, the notion that consciousness may be a function of brain complexity and increasing processing demands leads to a cognate position on the possible evolution of consciousness. One can suggest that consciousness will arise in complex brains to reflect the difficulties of dealing with parallel complexity and contemporaneity. Thus, consciousness is not an all-or-none phenomenon, but rather will arise in limited areas of information processing, such that mammals other than humans might be conscious of some limited, information loaded aspects of their cognitive processes, that infants may at first have rather limited conscious capacities when there are fewer processing demands,[162] and that adults with special skills and cognitive subsystems (as for example, pianist or mathematicians or jugglers) will have special consciousnesses related to those areas of thought and action.

Chapter 5

Aspects of consciousness

Attention

I have repeatedly made reference to the relation between attention and consciousness. It is now time to discuss the issue in detail. Notions of consciousness and attention have frequently been coextensive in cognitive speculations. The common usage frequently coalesces attention, analytic processes, and consciousness. It is said, for example, that one attends to the theme of a musical composition, to the message in a speech, to the colors in a painting. In contrast, I argue that the attention concept need claim only that one focuses on (obtains information from) the spatiotemporal source of the music, the speech, or the painting, that is, on general locations and occasions in one's internal or external environment.

Most theories of attention fall into two broad classes: early-selection theories and late-selection theories. Early-selection theories claim that top-down processes, sometimes called attentional mechanisms, select only parts of the perceptual continuum and inhibit or filter (exclude) others.[163] Late-selection theories admit all the available evidence to analytic, parallel (activational) processes and then select relevant aspects of the available unconscious evidence.[164] In both kinds of theories, there is frequently some implication that the selection process involves the use (construction) of a conscious state. Alternatively, one may define attention as being independent of consciousness and restrict it to the potential intake of formation. Attention is the process whereby a specific part of the space-time continuum is made available for further processing. As a result, the information potentially available in the spatiotemporal section that is scanned is accessible to all relevant analytic processes. Typically, conceptual (top-down) processes will select the analyses to be performed. Under some circumstances the nature of the information scanned may command analytic processes, as, for example, in the "attention" paid to a loud noise or bright light. As a result of spatiotemporal attention and the subsequent activation of selected cognitive representations, the structures (schemas) activated by these two processes will be available for the construction of the unified phenomenal experience. When the part of the spatiotemporal continuum that is selected by attention is very narrow and when the consequent activated schemas are determined primarily by the information scanned and by a (small) number of relevant schemas, the conscious contents will be determined and generally invariant from situation to situation and person to person (e.g., in the psychophysical experiment or by the demands of a specific noise or of a familiar word). There is no deliberate or "top down" selection in this view of attention, except for the primitive process that includes or excludes parts of the spatiotemporal flux. Selection phenomena and attentional priorities are determined at the next level of analysis and beyond, after the mere intake of the "physical," perceptual information from the spatiotemporal flux has taken place. Parallel (late selection) or serial (early selection) processing can then proceed on the given unanalyzed information, followed in most instances by conscious construction. For example, the request to "look for a red object in this room" does not involve a peripheral looking for red objects; what does happen is that the whole room becomes the domain of the spatiotemporal continuum that is scanned. Independently of this directive process, another top-down process will then select the evidence that fits the "red" criterion. Relevant evidence on this purely spatiotemporal selection by attentive processes has been developed in work on the "size" of the attentional spotlight.[165] In a sense, this is a combination of the early- and late-selection views. However, the "early" selection advocated here is neutral with respect to conceptual or semantic features. Most of the work that is appealed to by the commonsense notion of attention is done by late-selection mechanisms. In summary, then, we can recast "early" and "late" models of attention, not as competitive explanations of the same phenomenon, but as distinct stages and modes. Each of these "stages" addresses a different set of phenomena, and altogether these various processes constitute the general concept of "attention."

The arguments presented above speak to the steps at which information is "gathered" and to the possible conscious constructions that result from the initial activations. The selective nature of constructive consciousness uses the information most appropriate to the current task and goals. Such construction may be early or late; it may use serial or parallel processes. The concept of attention can then be reserved for the initial step in the information flow where specific spatiotemporal targets become the objects for further processing.

As early as 1973 Posner distinguished between attention, selectivity, and processing capacity, which was his identification of consciousness.[166] He maintained the distinction between attention and consciousness and differentiates between them. Thus attention is used for locating targets.[167] Similarly,

Daniel Kahneman and Anne Treisman have argued that "attention is assigned to objects, or to the locations that objects occupy, rather than to nodes in long-term memory."[168] In pain perception, modulation is achieved by shifting attention, and again the data suggest that this shift is pre-conscious and early in the sensory train.[169] And the authoritative treatment of attention written and edited by Pashler shows that, with little reference to consciousness, the broad range of phenomena often included under "attention" is to a large extent covered by selectivity, its control, and its limitations.[170]

This discussion clarifies the relation between attention and consciousness. Attention is a mechanism that determines the organism's spatio-temporal orientation to currently interesting or relevant events. The latter are of course exactly the events that lead to their selection as "important" by the consciousness mechanism. Thus attention will do some of the preliminary selection of events that will eventually appear in conscious states. It is not surprising that attention and consciousness are so often confused.

There is a remaining question that concerns so-called automatic vs. voluntary attention. Baars, for example, talks specifically about attention as controlling access to consciousness, which is — from my view — about half right. However, he posits that attention can be conscious or unconscious, and he maps that distinction into "flexible, voluntary access control" vs. "automatic access control."[171] The former is said to deal with emergencies and opportunities, the latter makes possible rapid shifts to significant events. I am most reluctant to enter a discussion of "voluntary" thought and behavior. For the present discussion it should be sufficient to say that we usually call those acts voluntary that are preceded by conscious events that require or intend the target act, whereas automatic acts have no such precursors. What this implies for consciousness and attention is that the spatio-temporal focussing is in the "voluntary" case initiated by some conscious thought, whereas in the automatic case no such conscious content precedes the attentional focussing.

If attention accounts for some but not all occurrences of conscious constructions, what about the others. There are nonattentional occasions when conscious events occur. The majority of these apparently occur when the general mental set is passive. I describe these nonattentional processes at greater length below under the aegis of mind-popping and similar phenomena. Essentially I would argue that the individual is either in a state of some active readiness when attentional processes are invoked or about to be invoked or in a passive state when a variety of activations and intra- or extrapsychic events can produce conscious states.

In summary then attention and consciousness are related because attention may lead to some conscious processes but that attention need not lead to conscious constructions nor does a conscious construction (see, for example, dreams below) need a prior attentional sequence.

Memory

The commonsense notion of human memory intrudes into psychological discussions by its insistence that consciousness is a necessary criterion, and that a "memory" is a copy of some previous experience. In contrast current psychological knowledge asserts that memory is constructed out of available evidence, past experience, and current expectations. In the common language, memory and remembering usually refer to bringing into consciousness something that is absent or that has occurred in the past. Psychologists have, especially recently, also used the term memory to refer to any mental content that is produced, regardless of whether the subject knows or recognizes the production as being "memorial," i.e., as being relevant to some past or current intention or requirement. It is in this context that one speaks of unconscious memories.

Recall and retrieval

The most frequent emergence of memorial consciousness is found in the act of recall. Both the commonsense notions of recalling and remembering and the experimental procedures for recall require a conscious construction that is seen to be responsive to some demand or requirement. An important aspect of conscious memorial events is the fact that "memory" depends on organization, on the relations among the target event and other mental contents. Such principles as subordinate, coordinate and proordinate organizations provide the underlying, unconscious structures that generate conscious experiences.[172]

Recall typically requires a retrieval process that is often, but not always, indexed by waystations that appear as conscious. It is in recall that it is possible to obtain protocols in which people are able to describe such waystations, conscious equivalents of search processes, and — at times — attempts at recognition of the retrieved material. In recall a higher order demand or task specifies what are and what are not acceptable conscious constructions. Errors in recall are constructions that, while factually erroneous, still respond to some higher-order requirement, as, for example, in recalls that convey the gist of the message without being "correct" in the narrower sense.

Recognition

In recognition different methods and instructions will produce different conscious constructions. The underlying activation, usually expressed phenomenally in terms of familiarity, will emerge in different forms in the conscious constructions. The following discussion oversimplifies the recognition paradigm. I have presented a model involving both familiarity judgments and contingent retrieval which is currently in wide use.[173]

Consider first of all the most frequently used recognition task. Subjects are presented with materials, in part some that have been previously shown and in part relatively new, distractor items. As the subjects see or hear these items, they are required to say whether they have seen or heard this material before. In such a situation the presented material activates its representation and activation spreads to other related representations. If the "stored" material has also recently been activated, then "old" items will have a greater total current activation (and will be more integrated) than will "new" items. If some criterion is set for such levels of activation then the old items will usually fall above it and new items below. However, depending on the task and instructions the false alarms to new items may be as high as 50%.[174] This rather crude criterion of relative activation may be sufficient to trigger the "yes" and "no" responses. What is the current conscious construction? It will be in keeping with the instructions — "tell me which one you think you have seen before." The highly activated items are more likely to be experienced as "having been seen before" — the subject will, in keeping with the task and instructions, "have an 'old' experience." In actuality, the situation becomes more complicated when retrieval processes enter into the judgment.

As I noted in Chapter 3, a somewhat different decision is illustrated in the forced choice recognition experiment. Here the subject is presented with an "old" and a "new" item at the same time; the instructions — explicit or implicit — are NOT to say which looks old, i.e., familiar, but rather to make a specific "choice" between the two items. The underlying process — of differential activations reaching a level above or below a crude criterion — is much the same.

The subject produces the same kind of action but what is experienced is much more a sense of "having made a choice." Thus, subjects report that they are "judging familiarity" in one case and "making choices among alternatives" in the other.

Conscious and unconscious memories

In the 1970s and 1980s intense interest arose in a type of "memory" research that strains the commonsense definition. The work on lexical decisions, priming, and spreading activation makes distinctions among memory and other cognitive categories, such as perception, rather tenuous.[175] The fact that people perceive words more easily after having seen related items, that they make lexical decisions faster after having been primed, or that they can identify higher-order characteristics without being able to identify lower-order ones raises (unnecessary) questions about the extent to which the use of prior experience constitutes memory or perception. As far as consciousness is concerned, subjects in these experiments do not seem to be aware of the fact that some of their productions are related to prior experiences; they are unconscious of the connection. Activation may produce effects without any conscious registration when, for example, the indirect activation of words has comparable effects on a priming task and a recognition task.[176] See also the discussion of unconscious perception in Chapter 2.

Episodic vs. semantic memory

The distinction between episodic and semantic memory has heuristic value in distinguishing between autobiographical, episodic knowledge that is deliberately and consciously accessed, that is context dependent, and is "remembered," and general semantic knowledge that is often automatically available, is context free, and is "known."[177] Semantic knowledge is unitized and often represents the kind of qualitatively different structure that can be ascribed to expert knowledge. Episodic knowledge, on the other hand, may or may not be subject to such qualitative integration. Some episodic autobiographic knowledge seems to have automatic characteristics, and some general semantic knowledge requires contextual retrieval. In terms of the automatic/controlled dimension, the distinction between automatic knowing and deliberate remembering does not easily map into the distinction between semantic and episodic information. The distinction between semantic/general and episodic/autobiographic knowledge has obvious heuristic value, but little in the way of principled theoretical utility. Whereas automatic and nonmediated access describes much of semantic knowledge, and conscious access much of episodic knowledge, the distinction between the two systems is far from clear.[178]

In summary, the dichotomies advocated and the systems proclaimed may map fuzzily into one common characteristic, the use of the selective function of consciousness in achieving access to information. There are of course a number of other distinctions that these dichotomies describe — my only concern here is their common characteristic. The use and intervention of conscious processes is the result of specific tasks, demands, and intentions. Conscious processing is usually invoked for some parts of most memorial activity — it is not an all-or-none function.

Primary and short term memories

Distinctions among such concepts as short-term memory, primary memory, working memory, and consciousness tend to shift from time to time. Short-term memory and primary memory have been used interchangeably. Similarly, working memory is frequently used to refer to a blackboard conception, only partly similar to the limited-capacity notion of consciousness. On the other hand, some writers seem to use short-term memory as equivalent with momentary, limited-capacity consciousness.[179] I would prefer to use consciousness to refer to material that is phenomenally immediately available and needs no retrieval, whereas short-term memory should be reserved for the limited amount of information that is quickly retrieved, often with a very limited expenditure of processing resources.

I start with consciousness as the common ending point of all of these constructions. William James used the term "primary memory" to refer to the current contents of consciousness that are immediately present and need no "retrieval." Given the limitation of conscious capacity, one would expect all such contents to be limited to some five to seven units — the limits usually imposed on "short term" memories. Thus, one of the components of short term memory involves current conscious contents. Instead of postulating an additional short term memory system or "box," I use degree of activation to define other quickly accessible memorial contents. Assuming a rather steep initial decay of activation, material that has been presented or processed during preceding seconds can be quickly and efficiently brought into conscious constructions. Rehearsal may either maintain material within current conscious constructions or keep activation very high so that the material can be quickly brought into consciousness. In addition there are mental contents that are kept at relatively high levels of activation. I have referred to these as "state of the world" memories which contain information of who and where we are, what we are doing, and what our currently effective goals and plans are. Finally, the executive functions of short term memory (if any) are subsumed under the serial and prospective functions of consciousness. This kind of approach eliminates the need for different short and long term systems and brings short term and long term phenomena into a common theoretical framework.

Amnesia: A disease of consciousness

Research and theory of the past several decades has shown that the amnesic syndrome provides an excellent natural laboratory for examining current theories of memory. I want to argue that an appeal to the functions of consciousness provides the theoretical formulation for an understanding of the memorial disability that we find in anterograde amnesia. For purposes of this discussion, I shall restrict myself to the kind of phenomena typically found in the performance of patients suffering from Korsakoff's syndrome. Whether the same arguments apply to other pathologies of the mind is left open.

The central proposition is that the amnesic patient suffers from an inability to create new conscious concatenations, new contexts for old knowledge, or conscious access routes to information that is not available automatically. This confirms the particular functions of subjective consciousness that I have indicated previously. On the other hand some of the selective and serial aspects of consciousness are still available — the amnesic patient is not overwhelmed by too much or by parallel flooding of information. In short, the amnesic patient has a deficiency in conscious functioning which prevents the storage of new information or the retrieval of previously stored material, unless it can be done automatically and without the intervention of the conscious apparatus. What the amnesic patient cannot do is to encode and store "belongingness" — what goes with what — unless it is done automatically.

Various reports on patients with very dense amnesias have described the pathologies of consciousness. Patients describe themselves as being "prisoners of the present," as experiencing only "momentary consciousness." They still appear to be able to construct conscious contents as a function of current activations, when there is "bottom up" activation, or in terms of pre-traumatic automatically accessed memories. What they cannot do is to use or construct novel post-traumatic contents. Tulving has presented a case which illustrates this conscious inability, the failure to construct conscious contents. One extract of the interview has the interviewer ask what the patient will be "doing tomorrow." The answer is that the patient "doesn't know" and his mind is "blank" when trying to think about it. He is living in a "permanent present," and he cannot remember particular episodes in the past or construct possible futures.[180] In other words, he is unable to construct conscious contents about the past or present, i.e., concatenations of new or imagined events or of the present and the past. On the other hand, knowledge that does not require novel constructions is generally unimpaired.

"Facilitation through priming" is unaffected by the amnesic syndrome.[181] Priming operates without access to conscious mechanisms. The instances of the acquisition of new information or relationships are all examples of learning that requires little or no conscious intervention. It involves typically the acquisition of motor skills, perceptual relationships, or the achievement of new unitizations. All of these are, or can be, acquired automatically, without the intervention of subjective consciousness. In fact, one can demonstrate the automatic acquisition of complex skills in the absence of conscious participation. For example, amnesic patients can acquire computer routines without knowing (consciously) that they have learned them.[182] In other words, learning can take place with the serial, limited aspect of the system intact but without subjectivity. As I have noted in Chapter 2 animals who may also lack the subjective consciousness can learn efficiently with the limited serial system on the basis, for example, of conditioning mechanisms. And if amnesia is a disease in which the subjective aspect of consciousness is missing, it leaves intact the prevention of ideational flooding. That is a symptom of other diseases.

Amnesic patients have been demonstrated to be deficient with respect to new declarative, episodic, or explicit information (to use the terms used to describe the acquisition of information that requires conscious intervention). It is the case of course that amnesic patients can usually engage in some limited conscious elaboration, because their amnesias are rarely so dense, for example, that they recall nothing on a free recall test.

Dreaming, mind popping, and similar phenomena

Anecdotes abound about inaccessible thoughts and memories coming to mind with repeated attempts, after periods of delay or rest, or unintentionally when engaged in an unrelated activity. Two of these phenomena have been explored in studies of hypermnesia/reminiscence and incubation. Hypermnesia/reminiscence refers to the fact that people can remember more after a period of delay than they remember immediately after presentation of the material, and incubation described the improved ability at problem solving after periods of delay or rest.[183] The third (here called mind-popping) has received relatively little attention. In mind-popping, surprising and unanticipated mental contents are brought to consciousness when one is preoccupied with other irrelevant tasks or thoughts. Mind popping will be shown to be similar to the activations observed in dreams.

The most unusual conscious constructions occur in dreams. Traces of real world evidence mix with ancient and contemporary themes and with current conscious contents that, while often weird and novel, are still highly structured and certainly not random. Something constructs the consciousness that we dream. The mechanism that does the constructing and the material that is used are not different from the representations and processes that are responsible for consciousness in the waking state.

In the latter the evidence that arrives at the mental frontier, that activates schemas and structures, that generates and validates hypotheses, is itself structured by the reality and lawfulness of the external world. Rarely does our awake experience of the world violate the laws of nature or social usage. Both concrete and abstract schemas, generic ones and their instantiations, depend to a large extent on the current activation by the imperatives of a real world, peopled by real problems and real situations. There is something out there that demands attention, thought, and action. These thoughts and actions are determined and modified in part by previous activations, by schemas and structures that are still active as a result of our continuing transactions with the world; otherwise our actions would be ahistorical; they are context bound.

In dreams, however, present activations from the environment are of relatively little importance; we do not see or hear any surrounding scenarios. Although there is no doubt that some current activations (such as alarm clocks, sexual arousal, bladder pressure, and smells) activate their respective structures and enter into dreams, these occurrences do not make up the major part of our dream world, no do they usually provide interesting scenarios. Dreams are constructed out of the remnant activations of the preceding hours and days. These activations are of two kinds — generic schemas that have received activation from one or more sources and instantiated schemas (perceptions and thoughts) that are the result of specific experiences and thoughts in the preceding hours. But these active schemas are not organized by the structure of the world; they are the haphazard activations of a variety of experiences, some of them quite unrelated or even incompatible. They are available in varying degrees of activation for conscious constructions and, in many cases, will be activated structures that were not used in conscious constructions during the waking state at all. Without the guiding structures of the real world, these structures are now "free"; combinations of them that were not coacting in the face of evidence may now seek (activate) higher and more abstract structures that themselves may have been quiescent. Whereas my breakfast thoughts and my afternoon lecturing thoughts are not likely to have activated similar or overlapping features or structures, their remnants, their residues are still active as I sleep. And in my dreams they may find a higher-order schema or hypothesis that combines a bowl of Rice Crispies with the image of a student busily burying his notes therein. Similarly, abstract structures that have not been used for daytime constructions, because they produce unpleasant, conflicting consequences, may now well find conscious expression because the instantiations that they find are "disconnected" and unlikely to lead to conflict.

Dreams are therefore determined by two sources — activated remnants of the waking life and abstract structures that may or may not have been activated during the day or that are activated during dreaming. Dreams, too, are thus the product of top-down and bottom-up processes and are in principle no different from constructions in waking life.

Modern cognitive psychology has the tools to determine the nature of the residues that bring about strange dream combinations; it is less able to determine the themes of our dreams, the underlying major schemas that are used by, and that use, these remnants. The approach to the former might be similar to that used in the explanation of human error, but even that analysis still leaves open the question of why some potential errors and slips occur whereas others do not. That is the function of unconscious generic themes and schemas. The suggestion that the structure of the world is left out of the construction of dreams implies that dreams, in contrast to our consciousness of reality, are initiated by unconscious structures rather than by perceptual elements.

Finally, I want to mention the weird or peculiar characteristics of dreams, because they provide important clues to the occurrence of nonintentional thought. Dreams are conscious constructions that are independent of conscious intentions. Dreams come to consciousness without any intent on the part of the dreamer. I am primarily concerned here with the objects and actors of the dream, not with its meaning; I address the manifest content. The manifest content of dreams has long been known to be a reflection of our most recent experiences, of material of which we have been conscious shortly before. Both ancient and modern sources were well summarized by Maury: "Nous rêvons de ce que nous avons vu, dit, désiré ou fait."[184] The residues tend to include actions that have not been brought to a conclusion, unsolved problems, rejected or suppressed thoughts, and often mundane occurrences that have not been further attended to in the pressure of every-day life.[185] At the same time, manifest dream content frequently exhibits subsidiary and unnoticed "memories," as well as hypermnesic content, i.e., material that seems long forgotten. Thus dreams contain to a large extent recent activations, but not necessarily the most activated events of one's recent life. One of the apparent similarities between the manifest content of dreams and the instances of nonintentional thought (to be explored below) is that in both what becomes conscious or is dreamt is not necessarily, or even usually, the dominant preoccupation of the dreamer, perceiver, rememberer, but may be initially a rather peripheral event or object.

Dream theories that concentrate only on the residues in dreams fail to account for the obviously organized nature of dream sequences — however bizarre these might be. The notion that dreams represent residues of daily life has been voiced in modern as well as more ancient views about the biological function of dreams, which are seen as cleaning up unnecessary, unwanted, and irrelevant leftovers from daily experiences. The argument is that these experiential leftovers would seriously impair functioning, unless regularly removed or "unlearned." Robert, for example, in illustrating the "excretive" function of dreams, noted that one deprived of dreaming "would in course of time become mentally deranged, because a great mass of uncompleted, unworked-out thoughts and superficial impressions would accumulate ..."[186] Crick & Mitchison similarly note that the failure to remove (unlearn) undesirable modes of excitation might lead to "a state of almost perpetual obsession or spurious, hallucinatory associations ..."[187] It is very frequently this mental detritus that is used in constructing dreams. But the result is a coherent, but often weird, scenario, not typically just pieces of experience. Hobson's activation-synthesis hypothesis of dreaming[188] supposes that, apart from aminergic neurons, "the rest of the system is buzzing phrenetically, especially during REM sleep."[189] Such additional activations provide ample material to construct dreams and, as Hobson suggests, to be creative and to generate solutions to old and new problems.

In short, dreams are unintentional, they are constructed out of a large variety of activated mental contents, or of mental contents activated by a rather wide ranging process of spreading activation, and they are organized by existing mental structures.

Mind popping and the advantages of becoming passively conscious

Mind popping refers to the unintentional, usually completely unexpected coming to mind of words or other events that have no immediately distinguishable connection to the current scene. In the exploration of possible bases for mind-popping, I turn first to a phenomenon that has received relatively little attention in recent psychological research, i.e., the apparent facilitating role of preconscious mental content, and conversely the restricting role of conscious material. As an example, consider an experiment by Spence & Holland.[190] They presented the word CHEESE "subliminally" for 7ms or supraliminally for 2 s. They then presented a list of 10 associates of "cheese" and ten control words, followed by recall. Subjects in the subliminal condition recalled significantly more associated than control words, and more associates than the supraliminal group which showed no difference in the recall of the two kinds of words. Spence & Holland interpret the data as supporting Freud's notion that preconscious material "fans out" over an associative network to a greater degree than conscious material, which shows the "restricting effects of awareness." In other words, activated representations of which we are not aware produce a wider spreading than does "aware" material. The phenomenon is also relevant to the feedback function discussed in Chapter 3. If awareness restricts spreading activation then the material available subsequently will be less numerous and presumably more closely related to the initial state. That should improve problem solving and retrieval operations.

The phenomenon that "talking out" one's procedures and processes interferes with insight tasks is consistent with these general arguments.[191] Tasks that require unique insight solutions will, prior to solution, frequently yield reports of incorrect guesses and strategies. Such reports will activate continuing pursuit of erroneous solutions, and spreading activation will interfere with the activation of relevant appropriate structures and retrievals. On the other hand, in incremental, serial tasks verbal reports indicate waystations in the solution process and preferential, privileged activation of access routes that frequently lead to the correct solutions.

An interesting implication of this approach is that it is not crucial whether the individual is conscious or aware of the "subliminally" presented material. The important aspect is whether there is a conscious/deliberate attempt to retrieve the subliminally presented material. It is that process that seems to interfere with access. If the individual believes/asserts that he saw "nothing", then there is no deliberate search and there will be minimal interference with the underlying activation process.

In my discussion of the feedback function of consciousness I have noted that consciousness restricts and focuses subsequent pathways by selectively activating those that are currently within the conscious construction. That is the usual process during serial problem solving; mind-popping illustrates another process by not restricting possible solutions and permitting extensive (unconscious) activations that may lead to a solution. By mind-popping I refer to material (words, sentences, scenes, music etc.) becoming conscious without any conscious anticipation or intention by the experiencing individual.

In some examples of mind popping, the target is not intentionally sought out, it is preconscious, and thus has the characteristic of "fanning out," of engaging wider spreading of activation, and more extensive elaboration and activation. Thus "thinking" about something else makes it possible for the actual targets to become available for conscious construction. Interestingly, Taoism's wu-wei (possibly "non-acting") incorporates the notion of effective thought and decisions being dependent on a passive, nonactive attitude.[192] "Thinking about something else" is a defining characteristic of mind-popping. However, there are similar effects for deliberate retrievals (e.g., following delays in studies of hypermnesia and incubation) if the period preceding the retrieval is filled with material not relevant to the target task.[193]

Mind-popping occurs when there is no conscious intention to retrieve or access the target material. "Intention" in the wider sense invokes notions of intentionality, and the equation of intentionality with consciousness[194] is intuitively appealing, i.e., that a person needs to be conscious of an intention, as it is usually interpreted. The cases I discuss are occasions when the individual is instructed either to perceive, recall, or judge some event different from the actual target event, or to try to be nonintentional, i.e., not to try to perceive or remember anything in particular — reporting "whatever comes to mind." The cases come from a variety of different areas of investigation. The purpose of this collection is not to claim that the same mechanisms are necessarily operating in all these cases, but rather to demonstrate that the mind-popping effect exists and to suggest possible mechanisms.

In perception, Nelson was apparently the first to report a phenomenon sometimes called the anthill effect.[195] He noted that his awareness of what he thought were bits of gravel on an anthill was suddenly replaced by awareness of moving ants over a very wide area. He was aware of single ants, various orientations and patterns of the moving elements. Awareness of these movements and patterns was not possible when the gravel texture was perceptually dominant. The two kinds of percepts (awareness) alternated and the perception of motion was aided by stationary gaze and boredom. Any intentional tracking of the moving ants, however, terminated the motion percept. He concluded that the "focal percept" required task-oriented attention. His observations also imply that task-oriented attention eliminates the "peripheral" percept. A similar conclusion about the importance of a passive state for marginal "perceptions" emerged from the "subliminal perception" activity during the 1950s and 1960s

(See Chapter 3), which produced several reports of the importance of subjects being in a "relaxed" state in order to demonstrate such perception.[196]

Pervasive anecdotal evidence for the nonintentional effect in memory is found in the psychoanalytic literature. Brenner, among many others, has put it concisely: "… to the extent that anyone renounces conscious control over his thoughts, to the degree that he ignores his customary conscious interests, unconscious stimuli take over and control his thoughts."[197] Pine made the bridge between such psychoanalytic observations and the "subliminal perception" literature when he noted that the reduction of adaptive demands and of additional stimulus inputs makes it more likely that preconscious and unconscious material will emerge into awareness.[198]

In the area of priming and identification, there are a number of demonstrations. I refer again to Marcel's studies.[199] Subjects made judgments of graphic and semantic similarity for words that presumably could not be detected supraliminally. Semantic judgments were superior to graphic judgments, which in turn were more probable than correct "presence or absence" judgments at the low exposure rates. However, the effect was found only with subjects who "adopted a 'passive' attitude" and chose the words that "felt" right.

In Graf and Mandler we reported a case in which intentional search produced large interference effects as compared with a "passive" task requirement.[200] Subjects were given a list of words with instructions for nonsemantic processing. Following this presentation, the subjects were shown the initial three letters, i.e., the stems of the words, together with an equal number of stems unrelated to the presentation list. Subjects who were told to complete the stems with words they had just seen, the intentional group, completed 7.8% of the target stems with words from the presentation list, whereas a group who were told to complete the stems with the first words that came to mind, the nonintentional ("passive") group, completed 20.0% of the target stems with list words. In another study, we found the effect of conditional access to categorical information only under conditions in which subjects did not intentionally attempt to make categorical or perceptual decisions.[201]

There are occasional neuropsychological observations that imply interference due to goal directed activity and the advantage of passivity. Coslett and Saffran have presented data on patients with "pure alexia" who are unable to identify briefly presented words, but performed above chance on lexical decision and forced-choice categorization tasks.[202] The latter "implicit" access is in apparent contradiction to these patients' usual letter-by-letter technique for reading words. The implicit access improved when subjects were encouraged to develop a "feel" or intuition for the words, and to inhibit the letter-by-letter approach. Weiskrantz reported that some blindsight subjects have refused to "play the guessing game," and that "[i]f the subject is pressed … to be a 'conscientious' subject, he may fail …"[203] Marcel reports an observation of a blindsighted patient who was tested for spatial frequency resolution. Frequency sensitivity in the blindfield was better when the patient was distracted by conversation than when not so distracted.[204]

Why does intentional consciousness restrict the utilization of unconscious material? One possible explanation is a relatively simple interference notion. Consider a search process for somebody's name. The immediately obvious conscious contents are replete with the bringing to mind of possible names, of contexts in which one has seen the person, and so forth. All of these incorrect "thoughts" will provide activation to their underlying representations, which in turn will be the dominant preconscious material available for conscious constructions. The result is the well-known but little researched "looping" effect, in which the incorrect solutions repeatedly come to mind.[205] In the context of tip-of-the-tongue experiences, these incorrect intrusions have been called blockers or interlopers that "block" access to the target words.[206] If, however, material totally irrelevant to the task is the primary occupation of conscious constructions, there may be little interference with the mental structure initiated by the relevant task. The unconscious activation process, on the other hand, is presumably continuing without such constraints.

All of these processes may, of course, be operating at different times or at the same time, or some might be specific to certain instances of mind-popping. However, I want to argue that the most likely explanation for the advantages of a passive "nonconscious" state can be found in my initial considerations. When an individual is passive with respect to the current scene or world, when there is no current "problem" to be addressed, then there are no selective influences operating on the currently active unconscious representations. In other words, the "basic" aspects of consciousness are allowed to operate without conscious thought generating interfering cognitive states — we then operate at a more primitive subjectively nonconscious "cognitive" level.

There remains the question of why and how ideas come to mind at unprepared, nondeliberate times in the continuing thought process. Empirical evidence suggests that it is in part the result of intra- and extrapsychic priming, though often of a rather long term nature, and partly a function of passivity. Given that the increased activation and elaboration produce a fairly well activated and integrated "solution," why does it come to mind at a particular time? When the material that "pops" is relevant to some prior and abandoned problem then the "popping" is probably due to the problem being in a continuing high state of activation, and autonomous processes combine fortuitous and haphazard events (both extra- and intrapsychic) that become cues or primes for the solution that is now readily accessible.

I conclude that many, indeed most, of our perceptions and memories come to mind unbidden and not intended in the usual sense. Thus requirements or demands need not be conscious intentions. And a passive attitude may reduce explicit or implicit problem solving to a more simple unconscious process.

Imagery and consciousness

One of the most ubiquitous aspects of common consciousness is our ability to engage in conscious imagery. Imagery can be mundane or spectacular; it can occur without special effort or be the result of rather intense effort. It also occurs in a variety of sensory modalities. However, both common and psychological usage have shown occasional tendencies to use the term "image" to refer exclusively to visual imagery. This exclusive use of "image"is due in part to the mishap that befell the German word "*Vorstellung*" in its translation across the Atlantic around the turn of the century. In particular, it led to a sometime misunderstanding of the notion of "imageless thought." The report that associative and judgmental processes at times proceeded without intervening conscious contents was crucial for the development of a modern understanding of mental operations. The missing "images" were auditory or visual or kinesthetic, replaced by nothing or by contentless conscious experiences. In other words, what was discovered was the notion of "thought without conscious contents."[207] If that is so, what is a psychology of imagery about? It is a psychology of conscious processes. The generality of such a use of "image" becomes even more apparent when we consider a definition of imagery. There are essentially two very distinct aspects of the term "image." Stephen Kosslyn's definition includes them both when he notes that "an image is a representation in the mind that gives rise to the experience of 'seeing' in the absence of the appropriate visual stimulation from the eyes."[208] Kosslyn restricts himself here to visual images. However, the definition applies *pari passu* to the other senses as well; all that needs to be done is to replace "seeing, visual, and eyes" with "hearing, auditory, ears," "smelling, olfactory, nose," or "feeling, visceral, autonomic nervous system." In any case, we apparently are talking about a mental representation, and the phenomenal conscious experience of an image that is constructed out of that representation. How is that definition different from the definition of any other conscious content? The main difference is that some conscious experiences are constructed in the presence of direct activation from the event in question, whereas in the "image" case the event does not provide immediate activation. We can look at a Renoir painting or we can have an image of that painting in the absence of its physical presence. But note that such lack of direct activation from sensory stimulation is not restricted to visual or kinesthetic or auditory imagery; the lack also occurs during many of our reveries, whether problem directed or not. If we assume that imagery and "real" conscious percepts access the same underlying representation, one of the differences between the two is the clarity, distinctiveness, and intensity of the conscious experience. In the case of images, the representation is weakly activated, by other related structures or more generally by some conceptual top-down process; we may image a specific event or object simply by being asked to do so or because it fits a scenario in a particular imagined scene, or a dream. In the case of conscious percepts, the activation of the representation is direct; there is evidence from the environment that speaks directly to the representation. In short, we can treat imagery as a special case of the problem of conscious construction. Imagery generates conscious constructions in the absence of specific environmental evidence. The uses of imagery are therefore part of the uses of consciousness in general; imagery adds the advantage that the effects of consciousness can be made available free of contextual constraints. Imagery makes possible the construction of mental models and the mental simulation of past (and future) situations.

Chapter 6

Emotion and pain[209]

I devote a separate chapter to the problem of emotion for a variety of reasons. Whereas pain (and sometimes emotion) are frequently used as examples of qualia, emotion is one of the more complex categories of conscious experiences; it illustrates well the problem of schemas and the construction of conscious experience, and it is a topic with which I have been associated for some 40+ years. There is no intent to review the whole gamut of experiences and positions implied by pain and emotion. I shall restrict myself to a demonstration of how some aspects of these experiences are relevant to my discussion of consciousness.

Within the context of the theoretical ideas presented above, emotions and pain are particularly important because these are *prima facie* reactions to events and experiences of central importance to the individual. If attention needs to select anything and consciousness needs to elaborate it, it certainly would include pain and the emotions.

The varieties of emotions

Emotion is one of those common language terms about which the general speaker has little doubts but about which scientists of the mind find little agreement. I have long argued that emotion is not a consistent category, but I now introduce a witness from outside the field. William Ian Miller, a perspicacious lawyer and no participant in the emotion wars, has put it as well as anybody: "The literature on emotions still hasn't come to terms with whether there is a 'real' category that can include such disparate things as love, disgust, regret, boredom, but not sexual desire, pain, thirst or hunger. Few of us, however, who accept that there is a group of affects called emotions will agree on what to include; and emotion theorists' lists of basic emotions are as varied as are emotion theorists."[210]

So-called theories of emotion vary from those that ascribe simple conditioning models to the full range of animals to those that are tied to a romantic poetic appreciation of human emotions. The range includes such curiosities as a well organized and programmatic evolution of emotions, one by one, to neobehaviorist placing of preferences into environmental stimuli, to hot and cold emotions full of buzz and glitz. The most recent attempt, by Damasio, is too complex to permit extensive evaluation, with much dependence on selves and their consciousness, but its use of the James-Lange theory and the distinction between episodic and semantic memories ties it to the history of the field.[211] The range of human states considered by various theorists to be emotions range from sheer interest to rage, though curiously it often omits love and lust. A survey of the history the emotion concept shows appearing and disappearing symptoms over the past 2000+ years.[212]

Still, one of the most obvious conscious phenomena to which we refer in the common language is the experience of emotion and pain. Over the years these two categories have often been cited by psychologists and philosophers as exemplars of the operation of consciousness and qualia. And relevant to the construction of consciousness, pains and emotions are occasions of importance and relevance. The constituents of emotion and pain are prime candidates for achieving priority for conscious construction. I realize that such a position rules out the possibilities of unconscious emotions and pains, but I believe that emotions that are constituted in part of cognitive structures as well as autonomic reactions are unlikely condidates for unconsciousness. The notion of unconscious pain occurring in unusual cases has been broached by some anesthesiologists but is too controversial and complex to discuss here.

What is an emotion?

This was the question that William James posed over a hundred years ago and which has, on the one hand, had the beneficial effect of encouraging the study of whatever-it-is, and, on the other hand, produced a search for an answer to a pseudo-question. As behoves a well used umbrella term from the natural language, different people answer the question differently. Different people and different schools of thought wish to unpack "emotion" idiosyncratically.

William James established the tradition of unpacking common sense notions about the emotions, though in the process he misled several generations of psychologists into believing that his "What is an emotion?" admitted of an unequivocal answer.[213] James was primarily interested in the relation between emotional feeling and bodily expression. He criticized the received knowledge of the day which described emotion as a "mental affection" which "gives rise to the bodily expression." He thought that common experience suggests instead that our feeling of the bodily changes that follow the perception of some "exciting fact" *is* the emotion. Ten years later, James started to turn to the problem of defining the "exciting facts," a problem central to cognitive accounts of emotion but rarely, if ever, satisfactorily resolved. It is often forgotten that James argued that if all feelings of bodily symptoms were abstracted from the felt emotion, all that would remain would be a "cold and neutral state of intellectual perception." In illustration James noted that it would be impossible to think of an emotion of fear if "the feelings neither of quickened heart-beats nor of shallow breathing, neither of trembling lips nor of weakened limbs, neither of goose-flesh nor of visceral stirring, were present."[214] James was wrong in assigning the feelings of a particular emotion to a specific and preceding concatenation of visceral and muscular activities,[215] but his assertion about the centrality of visceral and muscular involvement has been ignored by many contemporary psychologists.

People seem to know full well, though they have difficulty putting into words, what emotions are, what it is to be emotional, what experiences qualify as emotions. However, these agreements vary from language to language and from community to community.[216] While the search for one general theory of emotion is probably in vain, it is possible to restrict oneself to what may be called the visceral or gut emotions, i.e., those that satisfy the requirement of visceral involvement. I suggested some years ago that probably the best way to look at emotion would be to generate some reasonable and useful theory that generated predictions and exhibited a range of competences that would overlap with common language uses of the concept.

My discussion will be concentrated on those emotions that involved some visceral, passionate involvement. The basis is the postulation of emotions as a conscious construction of visceral arousal and cognitive structures or schemas. However, since the common language often includes such states as patriotism, pride, satisfaction etc. as emotions I want to characterize the full range of the possible extent of emotion states. The cognitive structures involved in emotions are schemas or akin to schemas. These schemas are very similar to what are often called values.[217] Patriotism for example includes aspects of duties toward and appreciation of one's country. These value schemas can then be arrayed on a continuum of those that occur without integrated visceral arousal to those that are intensely "passionate." Thus, whereas patriotism and anger may be toward the ends of this continuum, states such as pride may be somewhere between these. I now proceed to a discussion of those states that do involve some degree of visceral arousal.

The construction of conscious emotion

The directing theme of my speculations about emotions has been the notion that emotional experience is constructed out of autonomic arousal and evaluative cognitions. The proposal for a constructivist view of consciousness provides that mechanism whereby these constituents can be combined into a single conscious experience. Subjective experiences of emotional states are conscious constructions that combine evaluative and arousal processes and structures into a single conscious experience.

The high-level structures that participate in this construction of emotion will to some degree be similar in different individuals, at least to the extent that we share a world and a biology that dictate fears, angers, joys, and lusts. Other integrative emotional structures will be highly idiosyncratic, at least in so far as we experience different loves, hates, and anxieties. Most important, the specificity of emotional experience will depend, as all conscious constructions do, on two general sources. The first will be the generic schemas that represent the abstractions that we have acquired in our lifetime — shaped by common human, cultural, social, and personal experiences. The second source is the instantiation of these general schemas with idiosyncratic evidence from the current surround, from cognitive states that represent value schemas, and from the autonomic nervous system.

The constructivist view of consciousness and particularly its sensitivity to intentional, situational factors is well demonstrated in experiments in which arousal is paired with values generated by environmental displays. Any evaluative states of the individual, arising from whatever source, will be used in the construction of an emotional state.[218] In any case, the constructivist approach does provide a principled account not only of how emotions are constructed but also of how the specific emotional experience arises out of the general characteristics of consciousness.

Common, natural (and philosophical) phenomenology has tended to take different emotional "packages" at face value. Psychology often merged with poetry in accepting as mental constituents, rather than *mental products*, such experiences as anxiety, romantic love, prejudice, beauty, jealousy and many others. The list of coherent emotions ballooned and, from an evolutionary point of view, new and more intricate "just so stories" emerged to justify the plethora of emotions. There was a flurry of attempts to unpack the emotions at the 19th century *fin de siècle*, but psychology soon returned to accept the phenomenology as the underlying reality. Obviously I take a position that is fundamentally different from the phenomenological approach. I believe that the attempts, originally by Husserl and in modern days imaginatively by Francisco Varela and others, may eventually bring useful information of the structure and operation of conscious states but they will not teach us how the necessary information is developed and consciousness constructed.[219]

It was not until some 10 years after the publication of his *Principles* that James turned to an understanding of the "exciting facts" and prepared the ground for the introduction of cognitive antecedents of emotional experience. At the same time the work in the late 19th century of John Dewey and Frederic Paulhan was generally ignored,[220] thus missing an opportunity to find some general principles that would make us understand visceral arousal, other than lists of occasions. The next half century was occupied with minor variations of James and/or forays toward cognitive/arousal positions that were not however taken seriously. The next big step came with Stanley Schachter's experiments (and his forerunner Marañon).[221] The flood of new positions on emotions, the increased volume of research, and the deluge of new theories followed Schachter's demonstration that cognitive and arousal factors could be experimentally separated in the production of emotional experience. During this period it was generally understood that no definitional problem existed, that we all know what emotions were. Experiments demonstrated what factors went into emotional experience — which we all "understood."

The cognitive part of the emotional construction has been various called appraisal, cognitive evaluation and other nouns modified by the adjective "cognitive." I finally settled for the notion of value as representing the central cognitive or valence component of emotion. Even the more simplistic approaches of basic emotions can be seen as valued or valenced cognitions. Even though these emotions have entirely different sources in the genetic and experiential history of the organism, they do all share their characterization as values. Sometimes these emotions are based on the similarity of external conditions as in the case of some fears and environmental threats in which case the value is one of avoidance and flight, sometimes they arise from incipient destructive actions which refer to values of hostility, sometimes from hormonal and physiological reactions as in the case of lust which maps into values and valences of desire, and sometimes from purely cognitive evaluations as judgments of helplessness that eventuate in anxiety and subsume such values as uncertainty etc. I would also argue that some of these "values" — that is bad! this is good! I approach that! I avoid this! — are genetically programmed. The human genome — as that of other animals — has incorporated consistent internal and external events into its evaluative repertoire. Other emotional "values" are experience-specific and explain changes over time within particular cultures as well as differences among different but contemporaneous cultures.

If values provide the quality of an emotional experience, then visceral activity, i.e., sympathetic nervous system (SNS) activity, provides its intensity and peculiar "emotional" feel. Unfortunately the occurrence of SNS activity is rarely if ever discussed in some principled way, when invoked it is usually listed as an accompaniment of emotions with little considerations of its conditions of elicitation. Most of the time we are given lists of occasions that produce SNS arousal, just as stress is defined by enumeration rather than by some behavioral or physiological principle. I have suggested a difference detection mechanism in which visceral arousal usually follows the occurrence of some perceptual or cognitive discrepancy or the interruption or blocking of some ongoing action.

The detection of discrepancies

One of the most important situations that organisms must confront throughout their life time is one of discontinuity of experience. Whereas on the one hand much of an organism's activity is devoted to finding out how the world works, to learn how find shelter and food, how to deal with its environment and its fellow beings, on the other hand it must be prepared for those situations where previously learned actions fail, where previously experienced situations are different. For some 30 years my candidate for such a principle has been the perception of discontinuity.[222] I propose the operation of a difference detector that detects events in the environment — or in the organism — that are different from what is organically or experientially to be expected, that detects the lack of efficacy or some behavior or action (the "interruption" of behavior), that finds no adequate response to some internal or external set of events, or that finds a situation more beneficial than expected — a "difference detector" that sets off SNS responses in preparation for action in response to a "different", i.e., unexpected, internal or external environment.[223] I would suggest that the discovery by LeDoux and others of a response in the amygdala to novel, threatening (i.e., "different") events, that is equally fast and also responds by activating the SNS, may well be the physiological counterpart of my difference detection mechanism.[224] And as I have suggested in Chapter 5, the difference detection mechanism is also important in bringing to bear consciousness-constructing mechanisms, as in troubleshooting, to the awareness of unusual and unexpected events.

I argue therefore that visceral emotions are generated by the experience of discrepancies, whether negative or positive, which release autonomic reactions, together with an evaluation of the situation which determines the quality of the emotion. But that definition also leads us to an understanding why emotions are such a frequent and obvious part of our conscious experience. If nothing else the discrepant situation is important to the individual, it is relevant to its continued well being and even survival. Thus, any situation which will arouse the visceral system will also set the stage for a conscious construction. As I have noted before most such constructions combine two or more components into a single conscious experience. Thus whereas the cognitions defining fear or joy or the operations of the sympathetic nervous system may be separately experienced, when they co-occur the primary experience is one of a single more or less intense emotion.

Aspects of emotion

One of the symptoms of the need for definitional clarity was demonstrated in the last quarter century in a feverish search for the basic emotions — the irreducible emotions from which all others are constituted. Apart from the fact that such a premise does contain the salutary notion that at least some emotions are constructed out of other basic ones, the general enterprise has bogged down in internecine warfare. Basic emotion theorists cannot agree whether there are 3, 6, 12 or even more such building blocks,[225] nor is there a consensus building; emotion theories are still procreating like rabbits. The fact that serious investigators can find such large differences in mechanisms and basic emotions suggests that a constructivist approach may well be the way out. Constructive approaches, such as the present one, can generate different emotional states, but also different circumstances for the appearance of emotion as idiosyncratic schemas change the character of the experience from situation to situation. Different emotion theories may well just emphasize one or another aspect of the constructivist scenario.

And yet, it should be obvious that a noncontested definition of emotion is not within our reach. And there is another reason why this should be — common language concepts have no unique scientific referents. But are there any discernable agreements? At least since Aristotle it has been argued that cognitive components are part of the experience of emotion and at least since Schachter's work in 1950s it has been generally accepted. With William James it has been agreed (by most, but not all commentators) that some degree of sympathetic nervous system activity is part of emotion. But, as I noted earlier it is possible to accommodate nonpassionate, quiescent emotions within a more general view.

The number of possible evaluative cognitions — across people and cultures — is innumerable. In principle any of a large number of valuative cognitions could result in an emotion, though cultural experience and environment constraints determine the number of possible emotional experiences an individual may have as a result of his/her background and experiences. I have already indicated the kind of general experiences and conditions that contribute to the cognitive components of such emotions as fear, love, anxiety etc. These are conditions that one finds in most all human societies and therefore we find emotions transculturally.[226]

The arousal component on the other hand is more constrained. Whereas it is possible that different cultures determine somewhat different patterns of SNS arousal, in general we are talking about the same hormones and the same effectors that produce the arousal that determines our passionate experiences.

If emotions are constructions that combine arousal and cognitions within the confines of conscious constructions then it should be clear that such constructions would preempt other conscious constructions, given the limited capacity of consciousness. I assume that the dominant importance of emotional situations will practically always call forth attentional activity and subsequent conscious construction. Under those circumstances we may assume that other conscious activity will not only be restricted but in fact impaired. I have discussed these issues at length elsewhere.[227] Of special interest is the effect of intense emotional experience (and autonomic arousal) — what we usually call stress — on human functioning and experience.[228]

One of my main aims has been to demythologize emotions. The poet and the philosopher may well wax lyrical when contemplating the throes of love or the terrors of fear or the ennoblements of patriotism, but the cognitive scientist must in the end accept that these are analyzable as concatenations of arousal and valued cognitions. We lose the poetry but I hope we gain in understanding and knowledge.

The construction of pain

Pain appears phenomenally to be a single sensation that varies in intensity and is accompanied, though apparently as a consequence and not a component, by visceral arousal. The scientific approach changed significantly in the 1950s and in 1975 I interpreted the existing evidence, following Melzack's and associates prevailing proposals, that two factors influenced pain — arousal and sensory stimulation.[229] I now want to argue not just what has since become a truism, i.e., that sensory and affective factor contribute to pain but rather that the affective contribution is truly an emotional one that can in turn be broken down into its components.[230] That is to say, pain becomes a function of sensory information, evaluative cognition, and sympathetic nervous system arousal — unified often in a single bounded conscious experience. There are a number of demonstrations available that show how manipulating or eliminating one of these factors changes the pain experience.

First the problem of changing the evaluative component. The valuation of unpleasantness that goes with painful experience appears to be at least in part modifiable. For example, restricted environments in early life seem to modulate degree of sensitivity to painful stimulation,[231] and prefrontal leucotomy also decreases the unpleasantness of pain without changing thresholds.[232] Restricting attention also reduces pain perception.[233] And as a general demonstration of the partial relativity of evaluative reactions, Zborowski showed some years ago how pain is perceived, interpreted, and evaluated differentially in different cultures.[234]

Second, controlling the degree of arousal. It is difficult to present a reasonable experimental situation. However, there are some suggestive observations: There is a phenomenon well known to pediatricians. Given an injection, an infant's immediate reaction (withdrawal, startle) is usually very fast (in the order of 200–400 ms) whereas the sympathetic nervous system has a latency of 2000 ms or more.[235] If one takes advantage of the gap between the two and distracts the inexperienced infant the reaction to the unpleasantness can be avoided successfully. Of course, once a child "knows" the significance of the hypodermic and its consequences this strategy does not work any more. There is also some evidence that drugs such as beta-blockers that reduce autonomic NS reactions may also ameliorate the experience of pain.

Thirdly, effects of eliminating the sensory contribution. How can we reproduce the complex that usually produces the pain experience while eliminating the effect of sensory pain? Is this just a thought experiment? No, it is made possible by an experiment of nature — congenital analgesia, the absence of the sensory pain experience. In recent years relatively little attention has been paid to this genetic disease. However the literature provides adequate evidence that our thought experiment is indeed possible.[236] In one study of a child with congenital analgesia the affected child reacted to being spanked with tears (arousal) and dismay (evaluation) even though it obviously could not experience any sensory pain.[237]

I would have liked to have more examples of this kind of deconstruction of emotion, and I only tangentially point to the effect of hypnotic manipulations of consciousness on emotional and pain perception because the example of pain applies to all true emotions. In any case deconstruction may not prove but it strongly supports construction as a basic principle.

I summarize: Pain is constructed within a single conscious experience out of sensory, evaluative and autonomic events. It is a principal example of a reaction to important events and experiences, that is given a high priority in serial generation, and primacy in conscious experience.

Chapter 7

The uses of consciousness revisited

I now return to the question which motivated this exploration: What advantages does this picture of consciousness confer on the organism it inhabits? What are we able to do with it that we could not do without it? I do not think the additional abilities are either mysterious or overwhelming, but, like many changes to our evolutionary makeup, they increment our more primitive abilities. The proposed mechanism used just a few novel adaptations. It does create conditions for making internal search processes as efficacious as external ones; we need not scan the world in order to benefit from the various possibilities that surround us. It significantly speeds up decision processes and problem solving by adding information that might otherwise have to be obtained rather laboriously from the external world. The alternative to self-activation via consciousness requires additional searches, either of the environment or of stored information. Organisms not endowed with this conscious feedback mechanism or not yet able to take advantage of it are clearly more dependent on environmental information and very often on trial and error behavior. Infants, who cannot recall in the sense used here, show such dependence.[238] With regard to infant consciousness, it is presumably fairly unextended and probably neither the relevant action and event schemas nor the higher order task and intentional structures are available to the newborn.[239] Simpler animals develop strategies of increasing the activation of current alternatives in their attempt to solve problems, and I noted the uses of vicarious trial and error behavior (VTE's) in Chapter 2. Humans too are known to use similar strategies when unable to generate reasonable hypotheses about the current state of the world. The mechanisms that select the relevant and important from the many potential sources of information in the environment are central to an organism's ability to deal with its world. Momentary states of consciousness are the final step in the reduction of information that floods the organism. Having arrived at a view of mental representation that invokes an efficient and economical system of parallel distributed processes, we can invoke consciousness to provide us with a slow, restricted, and serial processing state. For example, when decisions need to be restricted to few candidates or when problem solving reaches a stalemate, consciousness provides a deliberate stage for further appropriate action. States of consciousness not only reduce the flow of information to manageable proportions, but also make sense out of what is available and make subsequent actions more adaptive. Most if not all our knowledge and previous experience is stored (available, recorded) in structures that are both vast and differentially accessible. Some distinction needs to be made between that information and what is currently being used, worked on, and accessed. It is to a large part that function that is being exercised by consciousness. If one were aware (conscious) of everything one knows, or even of everything that is relevant (closely related to) some current experience, one would be swamped with information and unable to act. It is possible that other useful functions of consciousness emerged as a consequence of the emergence of consciousness, and not as a direct selective adaptation. In particular, the relation of thought and language may well have been such a later development, in part because of the usefulness of language for summarizing and capsulating event and thoughts. It is certainly the case that the interplay between human conscious thought and language has overwhelmed our view of both of them, often asserting that one could not exist without the other.[240]

One of the adaptive functions of consciousness, though not necessarily a result of specific natural selection, is the function of consciousness that chunks and abstracts knowledge into serviceable units for the social communication of knowledge. It permits the communicator to restrict the message to its salient aspects, and it also makes easier the reception of a limited rather than over-inclusive "messages." In addition, it permits the participants in social communication (and the transmission of culture) to construct reasonably concise and common mental models of social knowledge.

To illustrate the importance of limited, serial conscious representation, I return to the thought experiment explored in Chapter 2. Imagine consciousness as it is, behaving as yours does, but with one — and only one — exception, namely its seriality. Imagine consciousness as a parallel machine that permits everything currently relevant (or unconsciously active) to come to consciousness all at once. You would be overwhelmed by thoughts, potential choices, feelings, attitudes, etc. of comparable "strength" and relevance. As you read a book all the characters and their implications would cascade in your mental life. Consider the story of Lord Nelson and Lady Hamilton: As you read of one their trysts you would also be aware/conscious of his victory at Trafalgar, his defeats in the Mediterranean, his anti-republicanism, his narcissism — and her eventual obesity, her Lancashire beginnings, her lovers — and her husband's interest in classical vases and volcanos — and ....[241]

A huge mishmash of associations and ideas would envelop you, and that discounts simple environmental events such as the chair you are sitting on, the lamp that illumines your book, and so forth. A "humanly" impossible situation. All of this would come in simultaneous snippets, still constrained by the limited capacity of the machine. In this account I have not relaxed the constraint of limited capacity. To relax that restriction too, to permit all unconscious content to become conscious might strain the capacity of the reader to suspend disbelief. But as I suggested earlier that kind of consciousness is closer to a god-like characteristic — aware of all of his children (including the merest sparrow). Can one really that easily move from humanity to deity — by just suspending seriality, limited capacity, and the current relevance of consciousness?

Notes

1. For more general arguments against the tenability of the radical reductionist thesis, see, for example, Gold & Stoljar (1999).

2. I add comments, reservations, and forebodings in brackets.

3. Miller, 1962.

4. Natsoulas, 1970.

5. Neisser, 1967.

6. See also Garner, 1974.

7. In a personal communication Neisser indicated that he did not believe that consciousness is a useful concept for a stage of mental processing and that his avoidance of the concept was deliberate rather than unconscious.

8. Schachtel, 1959.

9. Shallice, 1972.

10. Mandler 1975.

11. For example, Sperling, 1967.

12. Posner & Keele, 1970.

13. Posner & Keele, 1970.

14. Posner & Boies 1971.

15. Posner & Klein, 1973.

16. Festinger, Burnham, Ono & Bamber, 1967.

17. Mandler, 1962.

18. Posner & Warren, 1972.

19. LaBerge & Samuels, 1974.

20. Gallistel, 1974, 1980.

21. Mandler, 1975.

22. Miller, 1956.

23. Craik & Lockhart, 1972.

24. Craik & Lockhart, 1972.

25. Piaget, 1953.

26. See also Mandler, 1962.

27. Gray, 1971.

28. Adrian, 1966, p. 242.

29. See Mandler & Mandler, 1974.

30. Mandler & Kessen, 1974.

31. See, for example, Luce, 1959 and Tversky, 1972.

32. Miller, 1962 and Gray 1971.

33. Miller, Galanter & Pribram, 1960.

34. See also Vygotsky, 1962.

35. For example, Miller, 1956 and Mandler, 1975.

36. Ornstein, 1969.

37. Ornstein, 1972, p. 87.

38. See, for example Craik & Watkins, 1973, and Woodward, Bjork & Jongeward, 1973.

39. Ornstein, 1972.

40. Ornstein, 1972, pp. 119–120.

41. Ornstein, 1972, p. 136.

42. Mandler, 1996a.

43. For example by von Hartmann, 1869.

44. See Mandler & Mandler, 1964.

45. For a more detailed discussion of the psychology of the late 19th and early 20th century, see Mandler, 1996b, and J.M. and G. Mandler, 1964.

46. Boring, 1953.

47. See, for example, Donald, 1991.

48. Gould, 1993, Pp.320–322.

49. See, for example, Gigerenzer & Goldstein, 1996, and Gigerenzer and Selten, 2001. For an earlier, similar argument, compare Simon (1956).

50. Claparède, 1934.

51. Jaynes, 1976

52. Gleitman, Gleitman & Shipley, 1972.

53. Muenzinger, 1938.

54. The useful concept of working memory (Baddeley, 1989) is more complex than either primary or short term memory; it elaborates the necessary structures that need to be easily accessed.

55. Adrian, 1966

56. Dennett, 1991

57. I assume that attentive mechanisms, in the sense of environmental orientation, evolved much earlier. Even cockroaches "attend."

58. The term "exaptation" was coined by Gould & Vrba, 1982, to replace "preadaption." Both terms refer to the evolutionary acquisition of characteristics and features which is more

or less accidental, i.e., it serves an adaptive function carried along by some actual adaptive facture. While not immediately contributing to the organism's fitness it may well do so at some later stage in evolution.

59. And, of course, it would be easy to program a non-conscious computer to improve its performance by providing it with a limited serial output mechanism.

60. Cohen & Squire, 1980.

61. Gould & Lewontin, 1979.

62. Crick & Koch, 1990

63. Kitcher, 1990.

64. For a critique of the widely cited research with identical twins, see Mandler, 2001.

65. Kant, 1929(1781)

66. I enter the spirit of academic nitpicking by asserting the validity of "schemas" as the contemporary plural of "schema" in contrast to "schemata." "Schema" has followed the path taken by "dogma" and partly by "stigma" that has produced the acceptable "dogmas" and "stigmas."

67. Rumelhart & Ortony, 1978.

68. Rosch, 1978.

69. McClelland & Rumelhart, 1981.

70. Harrison, 1997; reprinted with permission of the author.

71. Parenthetically, I should note that there are several uses of "functionalism", the most prominent of which are the following four:

> *Functionalism$_1$* — the use most frequently adopted by philosophers and cognitive scientists — argues that the study of the "functions" of the organism (and its mind, etc.) can be carried out without reference to the underlying neuro-physiological hardware, typically by the manipulation of symbol systems and by complex computation. It is how the brain/mind functions that is of concern, not what its functions are. *Functionalism$_2$* is the simplest sense, and used in sensory psychophysics when particular mathematical functions are used to describe variations in experience as a function of variations of the sensory stimulus. *Functionalism$_3$* is best represented by the "functionalism" of the Chicago School of psychology around the turn of the century (Carr, Dewey, et al.). It was concerned with observable behavior, its effects and its evolutionary "functions." Its secondary emphasis of describing behavior "as a function of" some external events (e.g., McGeoch, and also the functionalism of psychophysics) can be seen as a forerunner of American behaviorism. *Functionalism$_4$* has been primarily used by linguists who wished to contrast their concern with interactive semantic, syntactic, pragmatic, social, psychological, etc. functions of language with formalist and modular views (e.g., Chomsky, Fodor).

My own approach comes closest to Functionalism$_4$, stressing various functions of consciousness, i.e., asking what consciousness is for, but without wanting to neglect its physical (physiological) representation — when appropriate

72. Marcel, 1983a.

73. Treisman & Gelade, 1980.

74. Posner & Boies, 1971; Posner & Snyder, 1975.

75. Posner & Snyder, 1975, p. 64.

76. Ericsson & Simon, 1980.

77. If it is agreed that the conscious product is not identical with the unconscious mental content then it is of course reasonable that such a modification requires other mental contents. However, these may be conscious contents.

78. Marcel, 1983a.

79. Bühler, 1907.

80. Thatcher & John, 1977.

81. Fowler, Wolford, Slade & Tassinary, 1981; Intraub, 1981; Marcel, 1983b.

82. Parker, 1977.

83. Köhler, 1929.

84. See, for example, Sheinkopf, 1970; Warrington, 1975.

85. Lazarus, 1981.

86. Head, 1920.

87. See, for example, Gregory, 1981.

88. The causal role of consciousness is, of course, otherwise obvious. When I have a toothache I first think of and then go to see my dentist.

89. For a summary of some of these phenomena, see Mandler, 1989.

90. Anderson, 1984; Johnson & Raye, 1981.

91. See, for example, Johnson-Laird, 1983.

92. Schneiderman, 1983.

93. Dixon, 1971; Dixon, 1981.

94. Eriksen, 1960; Holender, 1986.

95. For example, Dixon, 1981.

96. Eriksen, 1960, p. 298.

97. Dixon, 1971, p. 13.

98. Bowers, 1984.

99. Balota & Neely, 1980; Fowler et al., 1981; Marcel, 1983a.

100. Cheesman & Merikle, 1986.

101. For details, see Nakamura, 1989; for a summary, see Mandler, 1992b.

102. Graf and Mandler, 1984.

103. Nisbett & Wilson, 1977.

104. Green & Swets, 1966, for example, pp. 47 and 112.

105. Hamilton, 1859.

106. Miller, 1956.

107. Kaufman, Lord, Reese & Volkmann, 1949, and for an experimental analysis see Mandler & Shebo, 1982.

108. Iyengar & Lepper, 2000.

109. Dempster, 1981, p. 871.

110. Mandler, 1979; Mandler, 1980; Mandler, 1982.

111. Thagard, 1986, p. 313.

112. Jackendoff, 1987.

113. Flanagan, 1997.

114. Johnson-Laird, 1983.

115. Searle, 1983.

116. Searle, 1983, see also 1992.

117. Nagel, 1986; Griffin, 1984.

118. Van Gulick, 1988.

119. Strawson, 2000.

120. The section takes its title from a quote of Cicero's: "*Nihil tam absurde dici potest, quod non dicatur ab aliquo philosophorum*" (De Divitatione, ii, 58) Best translated as: "There is nothing so absurd but some philosopher has said it."

121. Before I start I note that a balanced view of the varieties of philosophical flavors, a good and sensible introduction, has been presented by Güzeldere, 1997.

122. McGinn, 1991.

123. Churchland, 1984.

124. Block, 1995.

125. Elster, 1999.

126. Hardcastle, 1995.

127. Baars 1988.

128. Shallice, 1991.

129. Shallice, 1972.

130. See for example Edelman & Tononi, 2000; Parvizi & Damasio, 2001. For an excellent collection of speculations about the neural basis of consciousness, see Metzinger (2000).

131. James, 1890, Ch. 5.

132. Cairns-Smith, 1999.

133. Humphrey, 1987, 1998.

134. Humphrey, 1998.

135. Macphail, 1998.

136. Quoted by Bernstein, 2001.

137. Nagel, 1986, p. 7.

138. See Dennett, 1991; Lycan, 1987.

139. For example, Skinner, 1964.

140. For example, Lycan, 1987, p. 132.

141. Nagel, 1986, pp. 19, 79.

142. See Putnam, 1960.

143. For example, Smart, 1959.

144. Lycan,1987, p. 44.

145. See also Dennett, 1978.

146. Van Gulick, 1980.

147. Sober, 1985.

148. See Cummins, 1975.

149. Churchland, 1981.

150. Gregory, 1981. I have considered this particular problem in the section on the feedback function of consciousness, which shows one way in which consciousness affects subsequent events.

151. Edelman, 1989; Penrose, 1994.

152. Deutsch, 1951, p. 216.

153. Searle, 1992, p. 18.

154. Lycan, 1987, p. 44.

155. For the young in body, the title goes back to an editorial in the *New York Sun* in 1897 in reply to an inquiry by a young reader. The editor reassured her: Yes, Virginia, there is a Santa Claus.

156. Searle, 1992, see also Crick, 1994.

157. Kinsbourne, 1996.

158. Baars, 1983; Baars, Fehling, LaPolla & McGovern, 1997.

159. Sherrington, 1933, p.22.

160. Weinberg, 1995, p. 39.

161. See, for example, Putnam, 1980.

162. But see J.M. Mandler (1997) for a different view.

163. Broadbent, 1958; Treisman, 1964, 1969.

164. Deutsch & Deutsch, 1963; Shiffrin & Schneider, 1977.

165. LaBerge, 1983.

166. Posner, Klein, Summers & Buggie, 1973.

167. Posner & Rothbart, 1992.

168. Kahneman & Treisman, 1984.

169. Miron, Duncan & Bushnell, 1989.

170. Pashler, 1998.

171. Baars, 1988, p. 302.

172. Current psychology has often forgotten that memory depends on organization and not on blind connections or associative "strengths." See, for example, Mandler 1967, 1968, 1977, 1979.

173. Mandler 1980.

174. Mandler & Rabinowitz, 1981.

175. Greenwald & Liu, 1985; Marcel, 1983a; Meyer & Schvaneveldt, 1971; Neely, 1977.

176. Mandler, Graf & Kraft, 1986.

177. Tulving, 1985.

178. See also McKoon, Ratcliff & Dell, 1986; Ratcliff & McKoon, 1986; Tulving, 1986.

179. Such as Ericsson & Simon, 1980.

180. Tulving, 1985.

181. Weiskrantz, 1985.

182. Glisky, Schacter & Tulving, 1986.

183. These will not be discussed further here but see Mandler, 1994.

184. Maury, 1878.

185. Freud, 1900/1975.

186. Robert, 1886, p.10.

187. Crick & Mitchison, 1983, p.114.

188. Hobson et al., 1987; Hobson, 1988.

189. Hobson, 1988, p.291.

190. Spence & Holland, 1962; see also Eagle, 1959; Paul & Fisher, 1959.

191. Schooler, Ohlsson & Brooks, 1993.

192. Watts, 1957.

193. Dorfman, 1990; Payne, 1987; Smith & Vela, 1991; Yaniv & Meyer, 1997.

194. Dagenbach, Carr & Wilhelmsen, 1989, and Searle, 1983.

195. Nelson, 1974.

196. For example Fisher & Paul, 1959; Fiss, Goldberg & Klein, 1963; see also Dixon, 1981, pp. 93–94.

197. Brenner, 1976, p. 191.

198. Pine, 1964 see also Koriat & Feuerstein, 1976.

199. Marcel, 1983b.

200. Graf & Mandler, 1984, see also Overson & Mandler, 1987.

201. Nakamura 1989.

202. Coslett & Saffran, 1989, see also Coslett, Saffran, Greenbaum & Schwartz, 1993.

203. Weiskrantz, 1986, p. 151 and passim.

204. A. J. Marcel, personal communication.

205. See Brown, 1988, for an example of induced spelling errors that keep recurring.

206. See Brown, 1991, p.216, for a review; Reason & Lucas, 1984, for relevant data.

207. Mandler & Mandler, 1964.

208. Kosslyn, 1983.

209. This chapter is based in part on a paper given at a conference on "Pain and consciousness" at Seefeld, Austria in August 1999.

210. Miller, 2000, p.36.

211. Damasio, 1999.

212. Mandler, in press.

213. James, 1884, 1890, 1894.

214. James, 1894, p. 193.

215. See for example Cannon, 1927.

216. Geertz, 1973.

217. Mandler, 1993.

218. See also Marañon, 1924.

219. See various contributions in Petitot, Varela, Pachoud & Roy, 1999.

220. Dewey, 1894; Paulhan, 1887.

221. Marañon, 1924; Schachter, 1966.

222. See my various books and articles on emotion, and also Cannon, 1930.

223. The mechanism applies to positive as well as negative emotions; see Mandler, 1990.

224. LeDoux, 1989, 1998.

225. Turner & Ortony, 1992.

226. But see Lutz, 1988 and others on non-Western emotions.

227. Mandler, 1984, 1997.

228. Mandler, 1992a.

229. Melzack & Casey, 1968; Melzack & Wall, 1965.

230. See also Chapman & Nakamura, 1999.

231. Melzack & Scott, 1957.

232. Barber, 1959.

233. Miron, Duncan & Bushnell, 1989.

234. Zborowski, 1969.

235. Peiper, 1956.

236. Fanconi & Ferrazzini, 1957; Sabouraud, Huchet & Turpin, 1968.

237. West & Farber, 1960.

238. See, for example, Piaget, 1970.

239. J. M. Mandler, 1984, 1988.

240. Revesz, 1954; Vygotsky, 1962.

241. With apologies to Susan Sontag's "The volcano lover."

References

Adrian, E.D. (1966). Consciousness. In J.C. Eccles (Ed.), *Brain and conscious experience*. New York: Springer.

Anderson, R.E. (1984). Did I do it or did I imagine doing it? *Journal of Experimental Psychology: General, 113*, 594–613.

Baars, B.J. (1988). *A cognitive theory of consciousness.* New York: Cambrdge University Press.

Baars, B.J., Fehling, M.R., LaPolla, M., & McGovern, K. (1997). Consciousness creates access: Conscious goal images recruit unconscious action routines, but goal competition serves to "liberate" such routines, causing predictable slips. In J.D. Cohen & J.W. Schooler (Eds.), *Scientific approaches to consciousness: The Twentyfifth Annual Carnegie Symposium on Cognition*. Hillsdale, NJ: Lawrence Erlbaum Associates.

Baddeley, A. (1989). The uses of working memory. In P.R. Solomon, G.R. Goethals, C.M. Kelley, & B.R. Stephens (Eds.), *Memory: Interdisciplinary approaches* (pp. 107–123). New York: Springer Verlag.

Balota, D.A., & Neely, J.H. (1980). Test expectancy and word-frequency effects in recall and recognition. *Journal of Experimental Psychology: Human Learning and Memory, 6*, 576–587.

Barber, T.X. (1959). Toward a theory of pain: Relief of chronic pain by prefrontal leucotomy, opiates, placebos, and hypnosis. *Psychological Bulletin, 56*, 430–460.

Bernstein, R. (2001). *Ultimate Journey: Retracing the Path of an Ancient Buddhist Monk Who Crossed Asia in Search of Enlightenment.* New York: Knopf.

Block, N. (1995). On a confusion about a function of consciousness. *Behavioral and Brain Sciences, 18*, 227–287.

Boring, E.G. (1953). A history of introspection. *Pyschological Bulletin, 50*, 169–189.

Bowers, K.S. (1984). On being unconsciously influenced and informed. In K.S. Bowers & D. Meichenbaum (Eds.), *The unconscious reconsidered* (pp. 227–273). New York: Wiley.

Brenner, C. (1976). *Psychoanalytic technique and psychic conflict.* New York: International Universities Press.

Broadbent, D.E. (1958). *Perception and communication.* London: Pergamon Press.

Brown, A.S. (1988). Encountering misspellings and spelling performance: What's wrong isn't right. *Journal of Educational Psychology, 80*, 488–494.

Brown, A.S. (1991). A review of the tip-of-the-tongue experience. *Psychological Bulletin, 109*, 204–223.

Bühler, K. (1907). Tatsachen und Probleme zu einer Psychologie der Denkvorgänge. *Archiv für die Gesamte Psychologie, 9*, 297–365.

Cairns-Smith, A.G. (1999). *Secrets of the mind.* New York: Springer-Verlag.

Cannon, W.B. (1927). The James-Lange theory of emotions: A critical examination and an alternative theory. *American Journal of Psychology, 39*, 106–124.

Cannon, W.B. (1930). The Linacre lecture on the autonomic nervous system: An interpretation. *Lancet, 218*, 1109–1115.

Chapman, C.R., & Nakamura, Y. (1999). A passion of the soul: An introduction to pain for consciousness researchers. *Consciousness & Cognition: An International Journal, 8*(4), 391–422.

Cheesman, J., & Merikle, P. (1986). Distinguishing conscious from unconscious perceptual processes. *Canadian Journal of Psychology, 40*, 343–367.

Churchland, P.M. (1981). Eliminative materialism and the propositional attitude. *Journal of Philosophy, 78*, 67–90.

Churchland, P.M. (1984). *Matter and consciousness: a contemporary introduction to the philosophy of mind.* Cambridge, MA: MIT Press.

Claparède, E. (1934). *La genèse de l'hypotheses.* Geneva: Kundig.

Cohen, N.J., & Squire, L.R. (1980). Preserved learning and retention of pattern analyzing skill in amnesia: Dissociation of knowing how and knowing that. *Science, 210*, 207–209.

Coslett, H.B., & Saffran, E.M. (1989). Evidence for preserved reading in 'pure alexia'. *Brain, 112*, 327–359.

Coslett, H.B., Saffran, E.M., Greenbaum, S., & Schwartz, H. (1993). Reading in pure alexia: The effect of strategy. *Brain, 116*, 21–37.

Craik, F.I.M., & Lockhart, R.S. (1972). Levels of processing: A framework for memory research. *Journal of Verbal Learning and Verbal Behavior, 11*, 671–684.

Craik, F.I.M., & Watkins, M.J. (1973). The role of rehearsal in short-term memory. *Journal of Verbal Learning and Verbal Behavior, 12*, 599–607.

Crick, F. (1994). *The astonishing hypothesis: the scientific search for the soul.* New York: Touchstone/Simon and Schuster.

Crick, F., & Koch, C. (1990). Towards a neurobiological theory of consciousness. *Seminars in the Neurosciences, 2*, 263–275.

Crick, F., & Mitchison, G. (1983). The function of dream sleep. *Nature, 304*, 111–114.

Cummins, R. (1975). Functional analysis. *Journal of Philosophy, 72*, 741–765.

Dagenbach, D., Carr, T.H., & Wilhelmsen, A. (1989). Task-induced strategies and near-threshold priming: Conscious influences on unconscious perception. *Journal of Memory and Language, 28*, 412–443.

Damasio, A. (1999). *The feeling of what happens.* London: Heinemann.

Dempster, F.N. (1981). Memory span: Sources of individual and developmental differences. *Psychological Bulletin, 89*, 63–100.

Dennett, D.C. (1978). *Brainstorms.* Montgomery, VT: Bradford Books.

Dennett, D.C. (1991). *Consciousness explained.* Boston: Little, Brown & Company.

Deutsch, J.A., & Deutsch, D. (1963). Attention: Some theoretical considerations. *Psychological Review, 70*, 80–90.

Deutsch, K.W. (1951). Mechanism, teleology, and mind. *Philosophy and Phenomenological Research, 12*, 185–223.

Dewey, J. (1894). The theory of emotion I. Emotional attitudes. *Psychological Review, 1*, 553–569.

Dixon, N.F. (1971). *Subliminal perception: The nature of a controversy.* London: McGraw-Hill.

Dixon, N.F. (1981). *Preconscious processing.* Chichester: John Wiley & Sons, Ltd.

Donald, M. (1991). *Origins of the modern mind : three stages in the evolution of culture and cognition.* Cambridge, MA: Harvard University Press.

Dorfman, J. (1990). *Metacognitions and incubation effects in insight problem solving.* Unpublished Ph.D. Thesis, University of California, San Diego, La Jolla, CA.

Eagle, M. (1959). The effects of subliminal stimuli of aggressive content upon conscious cognition. *Journal of Personality, 27,* 578–600.

Edelman, G. (1989). *The remembered present: A biological theory of consciousness.* New York: Basic Books.

Edelman, G.M., & Tononi, G. (2000). Reentry and the dynamic core: Neural correlates of conscious experience. In T. Metzinger (Ed.), *Neural correlates of consciousness: Empirical and conceptual questions* (pp. 139–151). Cambridge, MA: MIT Press.

Elster, J. (1999). *Alchemies of the mind: Rationality and the emotions.* (1st ed.). New York: Cambridge University Press.

Ericsson, K.A., & Simon, H. (1980). Verbal reports as data. *Psychological Review, 87,* 215–251.

Eriksen, C.W. (1960). Discrimination and learning without awareness: A methodological survey and evaluation. *Psychological Review, 67,* 279–300.

Fanconi, G., & Ferrazzini, F. (1957). Kongenitale Analgie: Kongenitale generalisierte Schmerzindifferenz. *Helvetica Paediatrica Acta, 12,* 79–115.

Festinger, L., Burnham, C.A., Ono, H., & Bamber, D. (1967). Efference and the conscious experience of perception. *Journal of Experimental Psychology Monograph, 74(4).*

Fisher, C., & Paul, I.H. (1959). The effect of subliminal visual stimulation on imagery and dreams: A validation study. *Journal of the American Psychoanalytic Association, 7,* 35–83.

Fiss, H., Goldberg, F., & Klein, G.S. (1963). Effects of subliminal stimulation on imagery and discrimination. *Perceptual and Motor Skills, 17,* 31–44.

Flanagan, O. (1997). Conscious inessentialism and the epiphenomenalist suspicion. In N. Block, O. Flanagan, & G. Güzeldere (Eds.), *The nature of consciousness: Philosophical debates* (pp. 357–373). Cambridge, MA: MIT Press.

Fowler, C.A., Wolford, G., Slade, R., & Tassinary, L. (1981). Lexical access with and without awareness. *Journal of Experimental Psychology: General, 110,* 341–362.

Freud, S. (1975[1900]). The interpretation of dreams, *The Standard Edition of the Complete Psychological Works of Sigmund Freud* . London: Hogarth Press.

Gallistel, C.R. (1974). Motivation as central organizing process: The psychophysical approach to its functional and neurophysiological analysis. In J.K. Cole & T.B. Sonderegger (Eds.), *Nebraska symposium on motivation: 1974* . Lincoln, Neb: University of Nebraska Press.

Gallistel, C.R. (1980). *The organization of action: A new synthesis.* Hillsdale, N.J.: Lawrence Erlbaum Associates.

Garner, W.R. (1974). *The processing of information and structure.* Hillsdale, N.J.: Lawrence Erlbaum Associates.

Geertz, C. (1973). *The interpretation of cultures: Selected essays.* New York: Basic Books.

Gigerenzer, G., & Goldstein, D.G. (1996). Reasoning the fast and frugal way: Models of bounded rationality. *Psychological Review, 103*(4), 650–669.

Gigerenzer, G., & Selten, R. (2001). Rethinking rationality. In G. Gigerenzer & R. Selten (Eds.), *Bounded rationality: The adaptive toolbox* (pp. 1–12). Cambridge, MA: MIT Press.

Gleitman, L.R., Gleitman, H., & Shipley, E.F. (1972). The emergence of the child as grammarian. *Cognition, 1,* 137–164.

Glisky, E.L., Schacter, D.L., & Tulving, E. (1986). Computer learning by memory-impaired patients: Acquisition and retention of complex knowledge. *Neuropsychologia, 24,* 313–328.

Gold, I., & Stoljar, D. (1999). A neuron doctrine in the philosophy of neuroscience. *Behavioral & Brain Sciences, 22*(5), 809–869.

Gould, S.J. (1993). *Eight little piggies.* New York: W.W. Norton.

Gould, S.J., & Lewontin, R.C. (1979). The spandrels of San Marco and the Panglossian paradigm: A critique of the adaptationist programme. *Proceedings of the Royal Society of London, Series B, 205*(1161), 581–598.

Gould, S.J., & Vrba, E.S. (1982). Exaptation — a missing term in the science of form. *Paleobiology, 8,* 4–15.

Graf, P., & Mandler, G. (1984). Activation makes words more accessible, but not necessarily more retrievable. *Journal of Verbal Learning and Verbal Behavior, 23,* 553–568.

Gray, J.A. (1971). The mind–brain identity theory as a scientific hypothesis. *Philosophical Quarterly, 21,* 247–252.

Green, D.M., & Swets, J.A. (1966). *Signal detection theory and psychophysics.* New York: Wiley.

Greenwald, A.G., & Liu, T.J. (1985). Limited unconscious processing of meaning. *Bulletin of the Psychonomic Society, 23,* 292.

Gregory, R.L. (1981). *Mind in science.* New York: Cambridge University Press.

Griffin, D.R. (1984). Animal thinking. *American Scientist, 72,* 456–464.

Güzeldere, G. (1997). The many faces of consciousness: A field guide. In N. Block, O. Flanagan, & G. Güzeldere (Eds.), *The nature of consciousness: Philosophical debates* (pp. 1–67). Cambridge, MA: MIT Press.

Hamilton, W. (1859). *Lectures on metaphysics and logic.* Edinburgh: Blackwood.

Hardcastle, V.G. (1995). *Locating consciousness.* Amsterdam: John Benjamins.

Harrison, C.J. (1997). The "Binding Problem" — an interdisciplinary issue. *Electronic publication.*

Hartmann, E. v. (1869). *Philosophie des Unbewussten.* Berlin: Duncker.

Head, H. (1920). *Studies in neurology.* London: Kegan Paul.

Hobson, J.A. (1988). *The dreaming brain.* New York: Basic Books.

Hobson, J.A., Hoffman, S.A., Helfand, R., & Kostner, D. (1987). Dream bizarreness and the activation-synthesis hypothesis. *Human Neurobiology, 6,* 157–164.

Holender, D. (1986). Semantic activation without conscious identification in dichotic listening, parafoveal vision, and visual masking. *Behavioral and Brain Sciences, 9,* 1–66.

Humphrey, N. (1987). *The uses of consciousness (James Arthur Memorial Lecture).*, New York.

Humphrey, N. (1998). Cave Art, Autism, and the Evolution of the Human Mind. *Cambridge Archaeological Journal, 8*(2), 165–191.

Intraub, H. (1981). Identification and processing of briefly glimpsed visual scenes. In D.F. Fisher, R.A. Monty, & J.W. Senders (Eds.), *Eye movements: Cognition and visual perception* . Hillsdale, N.J.: Lawrence Erlbaum Associates.

Iyengar, S.S., & Lepper, M.R. (2000). When choice is demotivating: Can one desire too much of a good thing? *Journal of Personality & Social Psychology,* 79, 995–1000.

Jackendoff, R. (1987). *Consciousness and the computational mind.* Cambridge, Mass.: MIT Press.

James, W. (1884). What is an emotion? *Mind, 9,* 188–205.

James, W. (1890). *The principles of psychology.* New York: Holt.

James, W. (1894). The physical basis of emotion. *Psychological Review, 1,* 516–529.

Jaynes, J. (1976). *The origin of consciousness in the breakdown of the bicameral mind.* Boston: Houghton Mifflin.

Johnson, M.K., & Raye, C.L. (1981). Reality monitoring. *Psychological Review, 88*, 67–85.

Johnson-Laird, P. (1983). *Mental models.* Cambridge: Cambridge University Press.

Kahneman, D., & Treisman, A. (1984). Changing views of attention and automaticity. In R. Parasuraman & D.R. Davies (Eds.), *Varieties of attention* (pp. 29–61). New York: Academic Press.

Kant, I. (1929[1781]). *Critique of pure reason.* London: Macmillan, 1929.

Kaufman, E.L., Lord, M.W., Reese, T.W., & Volkmann, J. (1949). The discrimination of visual number. *American Journal of Psychology, 62*, 498–525.

Kinsbourne, M. (1996). What qualifies a representation for a role in consciousness? In J.D. Cohen & J.W. Schooler (Eds.), *Scientific approaches to consciousness: The Twentyfifth Annual Carnegie Symposium on Cognition*. Hillsdale, NJ: Lawrence Erlbaum Associates.

Kitcher, P. (1990). Developmental decomposition and the future of human behavioral ecology. *Philosophy of Science, 57*, 96–117.

Köhler, W. (1929). *Gestalt psychology.* New York: Liveright.

Koriat, A., & Feuerstein, N. (1976). The recovery of incidentally acquired information. *Acta Psychologica, 40*, 463–474.

Kosslyn, S.M. (1983). *Ghosts in the mind's machine.* New York: Norton.

LaBerge, D. (1983). Spatial extent of attention to letters and words. *Journal of Experimental Psychology: Human Perception and Performance, 9*, 371–379.

LaBerge, D., & Samuels, S.J. (1974). Toward a theory of automatic information processing in reading. *Cognitive Psychology, 6*, 293–323.

Lazarus, R.S. (1981). A cognitivist's reply to Zajonc on emotion and cognition. *American Psychologist, 36*, 222–223.

LeDoux, J. (1998). Fear and the brain: Where have we been, and where are we going? *Biological Psychiatry, 44*(12), 1229–1238.

LeDoux, J.E. (1989). Cognitive-emotional interactions in the brain. *Cognition and Emotion, 3*, 267–289.

Luce, R.D. (1959). *Individual choice behavior: A theoretical analysis.* New York: Wiley.

Lutz, C. (1988). *Unnatural emotions: Everyday sentiments on a Micronesian atoll and their challenge to Western theory.* Chicago: University of Chicago Press.

Lycan, W.G. (1987). *Consciousness.* Cambridge, MA: MIT Press.

Macphail, E.M. (1998). *The evolution of consciousness.* New York: Oxford University Press.

Mandler, G. (1962). From association to structure. *Psychological Review, 69*, 415–427.

Mandler, G. (1967). Organization and memory. In K.W. Spence & J.T. Spence (Eds.), *The psychology of learning and motivation: Advances in research and theory* (pp. 328–372). New York: Academic Press.

Mandler, G. (1968). Organized recall: Individual functions. *Psychonomic Science, 13*, 235–236.

Mandler, G. (1975). Memory storage and retrieval: Some limits on the reach of attention and consciousness. In P.M.A. Rabbitt & S. Dornic (Eds.), *Attention and performance V*. London: Academic Press.

Mandler, G. (1977). Commentary on "Organization and memory". In G.H. Bower (Ed.), *Human memory: Basic processes* (pp. 297–308). New York: Academic Press.

Mandler, G. (1979). Organization, memory, and mental structures. In C.R. Puff (Ed.), *Memory organization and structure*. New York: Academic Press.

Mandler, G. (1980). Recognizing: The judgment of previous occurrence. *Psychological Review, 87*, 252–271.

Mandler, G. (1982). The integration and elaboration of memory structures. In F. Klix, J. Hoffmann, & E. v. d. Meer (Eds.), *Cognitive research in psychology*. Amsterdam: North Holland.

Mandler, G. (1984). *Mind and body: Psychology of emotion and stress.* New York: Norton.

Mandler, G. (1989). Memory: Conscious and unconscious. In P.R. Solomon, G.R. Goethals, C.M. Kelley, & B.R. Stephens (Eds.), *Memory: Interdisciplinary approaches* (pp. 84–106). New York: Springer Verlag.

Mandler, G. (1990). A constructivist theory of emotion. In N.S. Stein, B.L. Leventhal, & T. Trabasso (Eds.), *Psychological and biological approaches to emotion* (pp. 21–43). Hillsdale, N.J.: Lawrence Erlbaum Associates.

Mandler, G. (1992a). Cognition and emotion: Extensions and clinical applications. In D.J. Stein & J.E. Young (Eds.), *Cognitive science and clinical disorders* (pp. 61–78). San Diego, CA: Academic Press.

Mandler, G. (1992b). Toward a theory of consciousness. In H.-G. Geissler, S.W. Link, & J.T. Townsend (Eds.), *Cognition, information processing, and psychophysics: Basic issues* (pp. 43–65). Hillsdale, N.J.: Lawrence Erlbaum Associates.

Mandler, G. (1993). Approaches to a psychology of value. In M. Hechter, L. Nadel, & R.E. Michod (Eds.), *The origin of values* (pp. 229–258). Hawthorne, NY: Aldine de Gruyter.

Mandler, G. (1994). Hypermnesia, incubation, and mind-popping: On remembering without really trying. In C. Umiltà & M. Moscovitch (Eds.), *Attention and Performance XV: Concious and nonconscious information processing* (pp. 3–33). Cambridge, Mass.: MIT Press.

Mandler, G. (1996a). Consciousness redux. In J.C. Cohen & J.W. Schooler (Eds.), *Scientific approaches to consciousness: The Twentyfifth Carnegie Symposium on Cognition* (pp. 479–498). Hillsdale, NJ: Lawrence Erlbaum Associates.

Mandler, G. (1996b). The situation of psychology: Landmarks and choicepoints. *American Journal of Psychology, 109*, 1–35.

Mandler, G. (1997). *Human nature explored.* New York: Oxford University Press.

Mandler, G. (2001). Apart from genetics: What makes monozygotic twins similar? *Journal of Mind and Behavior, 22*, 147–159.

Mandler, G. (in press). Emotion: A jungle, not a garden. In D.F. Freedheim (Ed.), *History of psychology*. New York: Wiley.

Mandler, G., Graf, P., & Kraft, D. (1986). Activation and elaboration effects in recognition and word priming. *The Quarterly Journal of Experimental Psychology, 38A*, 645–662.

Mandler, G., & Kessen, W. (1974). The appearance of free will. In S.C. Brown (Ed.), *Philosophy of psychology* (pp. 305–324). London: Macmillan.

Mandler, G., & Rabinowitz, J.C. (1981). Appearance and reality: Does a recognition test really improve subsequent recall and recognition? *Journal of Experimental Psychology: Human Learning and Memory, 7*, 79–90.

Mandler, G., & Shebo, B.J. (1982). Subitizing: An analysis of its component processes. *Journal of Experimental Psychology: General, 111*, 1–22.

Mandler, J.M. (1984). Representation and recall in infancy. In M. Moscovitch (Ed.), *Infant memory* (pp. 75–101). New York: Plenum.

Mandler, J.M. (1988). How to build a baby: On the development of an accessible representational system. *Cognitive Development, 3*, 113–136.

Mandler, J.M. (1997). Representation. In D. Kuhn & R.S. Siegler (Eds.), *Cognition, perception, and language* (Vol. 2, of W. Damon (Ed.) Handbook of child psychology). New York: Wiley.

Mandler, J.M., & Mandler, G. (1964). *Thinking: From Association to Gestalt.* New York: Wiley (Reprint edition: Westport, Conn.: Greenwood Press, 1981).

Mandler, J.M., & Mandler, G. (1974). Good guys vs. bad guys: The subject-object dichotomy. *Journal of Humanistic Psychology, 14*, 63–87.

Marañon, G. (1924). Contribution à l'étude de l'action emotive de l'adrénaline. *Revue française d'Endocrinologie, 2*, 301–325.

Marcel, A.J. (1983a). Conscious and unconscious perception: An approach to the relations between phenomenal experience and perceptual processes. *Cognitive Psychology, 15*, 238–300.

Marcel, A.J. (1983b). Conscious and unconscious perception: Experiments on visual masking and word recognition. *Cognitive Psychology, 15*, 197–237.

Maury, L.-F.-A. (1878). *Le sommeil et les rêves.* Paris: Didier.

McClelland, J.L., & Rumelhart, D.E. (1981). An interactive activation model of context effects in letter perception: Part 1. An account of basic findings. *Psychological Review, 88*, 375–407.

McGinn, C. (1991). *The problem of consciousness.* Oxford: Basil Blackwell.

McKoon, G., Ratcliff, R., & Dell, G.S. (1986). A critical evaluation of the semantic-episodic distinction. *Journal of Experimental Psychology: Learning, Memory, and Cognition, 12*, 295–306.

Melzack, R., & Casey, K.L. (1968). Sensory, motivational, and central control of pain: A new conceptual model. In D.L. Kenshalo (Ed.), *The skin sense*. Springfield, Ill.: Charles Thomas.

Melzack, R., & Scott, T.H. (1957). The effects of early experience on the response of pain. *Journal of Comparative Psychology, 50*, 155–161.

Melzack, R., & Wall, P.D. (1965). Pain mechanisms: A new theory. *Science, 150*, 971–979.

Metzinger, T. (Ed.) (2000). *Neural correlates of consciousness: Empirical and conceptual questions.* Cambridge, MA: MIT Press.

Meyer, D.E., & Schvaneveldt, R.W. (1971). Facilitation in recognizing pairs of words: Evidence of a dependence between retrieval operations. *Journal of Experimental Psychology, 90*, 227–234.

Miller, G.A. (1956). The magical number seven, plus or minus two: Some limits on our capacity for processing information. *Psychological Review, 63*, 81–97.

Miller, G.A. (1962). *Psychology: The science of mental life.* New York: Harper and Row.

Miller, G.A., Galanter, E.H., & Pribram, K. (1960). *Plans and the structure of behavior.* New York: Holt.

Miller, W.I. (2000, 10 August 2000). Proverbs. *London Review of Books, 22*, 36–37.

Miron, D., Duncan, G.H., & Bushnell, M.C. (1989). Effects of attention on the intensity and unpleasantness of thermal pain. *Pain, 39*(3), 345–352.

Muenzinger, K.F. (1938). Vicarious trial and error at a point of choice. I. A general survey of its relation to learning efficiency. *Journal of Genetic Psychology, 53*, 75–86.

Nagel, T. (1986). *The view from nowhere.* New York: Oxford University Press.

Nakamura, Y. (1989). *Explorations in implicit perceptual processing: Studies of preconscious information processing.* Unpublished Ph.D. Thesis, University of California, San Diego, La Jolla, CA.

Natsoulas, T. (1970). Concerning introspective "knowledge". *Psychological Bulletin, 73,* 89–111.

Neely, J.H. (1977). Semantic priming and retrieval from lexical memory: Roles of inhibitionless spreading activation and limited-capacity attention. *Journal of Experimental Psychology: General, 106,* 226–254.

Neisser, U. (1967). *Cognitive psychology.* New York: Appleton-Century-Crofts.

Nelson, J.I. (1974). Motion sensitivity in peripheral vision. *Perception, 3,* 151–152.

Nisbett, R.E., & Wilson, T.D. (1977). Telling more than we can know: Verbal reports on mental processes. *Psychological Review, 84,* 231–259.

Ornstein, R.E. (1969). *On the experience of time.* Harmondsworth: Penguin.

Ornstein, R.E. (1972). *The psychology of consciousness.* San Francisco: Freeman.

Overson, C., & Mandler, G. (1987). Indirect word priming in connected semantic and phonological contexts. *Bulletin of the Psychonomic Society, 25,* 229–232.

Parker, R.E. (1977). *The encoding of information in complex pictures.* Unpublisheed doctoral dissertation, University of California, San Diego, La Jolla, CA

Parvizi, J., & Damasio, A. (2001). Consciousness and the brainstem. *Cognition, 79*(1–2), 135–159.

Pashler, H.E. (1998). *The psychology of attention.* Cambridge, MA: MIT Press.

Paul, I.H., & Fisher, C. (1959). Subliminal visual stimulation: A study of its influence on subsequent images and dreams. *Journal of Nervous and Mental Diseases, 129,* 315–340.

Paulhan, F. (1887). *Les phénomènes affectifs et les lois de leur apparition.* Paris: F. Alcan.

Payne, D.G. (1987). Hypermnesia and reminiscence in recall: A historical and empirical review. *Psychological Bulletin, 101,* 5–27.

Peiper, A. (1956). *Die Eigenart der kindlichen Hirntätigkeit.* Leipzig: Thieme.

Penrose, R. (1994). *Shadows of the mind: A search for the missing science of consciousness.* New York: Oxford University Press.

Petitot, J., Varela, F.J., Pachoud, B., & Roy, J.-M. (Eds.). (1999). *Naturalizing phenomenology: Issues in contemporary phenomenology and cognitive science.* Stanford, CA: Stanford University Press.

Piaget, J. (1953). *The origin of intelligence in the child.* London: Routledge and Kegan Paul.

Piaget, J. (1970). Piaget's theory. In P. Mussen (Ed.), *Carmichael's manual of child psychology*. New York: Wiley.

Pine, F. (1964). The bearing of psychoanalytic theory on selected issues in research on marginal stimuli. *Journal of Nervous and Mental Diseases, 138,* 68–75.

Posner, M.I., & Boies, S.J. (1971). Components of attention. *Psychological Review, 78,* 391–408.

Posner, M.I., & Keele, S.W. (1970). *Time and space as measures of mental operations.* Paper presented at the American Psychological Association Annual Meeting.

Posner, M.I., Klein, R., Summers, J., & Buggie, S. (1973). On the Selection of Signals. *Memory & Cognition, 1,* 2–12.

Posner, M.I., & Klein, R.M. (1973). On the functions of consciousness. In S. Kornblum (Ed.), *Attention and performance IV* (pp. 21–36). New York: Academic Press.

Posner, M. I., & Rothbart, M. K. (1992). Attentional mechanisms and conscious experience. In A. D. Milner & M. D. Rugg (Eds.), *The neuropsychology of consciousness* (pp. 91–111). London: Academic Press, Inc.

Posner, M. I., & Snyder, C. R. R. (1975). Attention and cognitive control. In R. Solso (Ed.), *Information processing and cognition: The Loyola symposium*. Potomac, Md.: Lawrence Erlbaum Associates.

Posner, M.I., & Warren, R.E. (1972). Traces, concepts and conscious constructions. In A.W. Melton & E. Martin (Eds.), *Coding processes in human memory*. Washington, D.C.: Winston.

Putnam, H. (1960). Minds and machines. In S. Hook (Ed.), *Dimensions of mind*. New York: Collier Books.

Putnam, H. (1980). Philosophy and our mental life. In N. Block (Ed.), *Readings in the philosophy of psychology*. Cambridge, MA: Harvard University Press.

Ratcliff, R., & McKoon, G. (1986). More on the distinction between episodic and semantic memories. *Journal of Experimental Psychology: Learning, Memory, and Cognition, 12*, 312–313.

Revesz, G. (1954). *Thinking and speaking: A symposium*. Amsterdam: North Holland Publishing Company.

Robert, W. (1886). *Der Traum als Naturnothwendigkeit erklärt*. Hamburg: H. Seippel.

Rosch, E. (1978). Principles of categorization. In E. Rosch & B. B. Lloyd (Eds.), *Cognition and categorization*. Hillsdale, N. J.: Lawrence Erlbaum Associates.

Rumelhart, D. E., & Ortony, A. (1978). The representation of knowledge in memory. In R. C. Anderson, R. J. Spiro, & W. E. Montague (Eds.), *Schooling and the acquisition of knowledge*. Hillsdale, N. J.: Lawrence Erlbaum Associates.

Sabouraud, O., Huchet, G. A., & Turpin, J. (1968). Neuronal arthropathies secondary to a congenital generalized analgesia: Congenital indifference to pain. *Annales Medico-Psychologiques, 1*(3), 468–469.

Schachtel, E. G. (1959). *Metamorphosis*. New York: Basic Books.

Schachter, S. (1966). The interaction of cognitive and physiological determinants of emotional state. In C. D. Spielberger (Ed.), *Anxiety and behavior*. New York: Academic Press.

Schneiderman, S. (1983). *Jacques Lacan: The death of an intellectual hero*. Cambridge, Mass.: Harvard University Press.

Schooler, J. W., Ohlsson, S., & Brooks, K. (1993). Thoughts beyond words: When language overshadows insight. *Journal of Experimental Psychology: General, 122*, 166–183.

Searle, J. R. (1983). *Intentionality*. New York: Cambridge University Press.

Searle, J. R. (1992). *The rediscovery of the mind*. Cambridge, MA: MIT Press.

Shallice, T. (1972). Dual functions of consciousness. *Psychological Review, 79*, 383–393.

Shallice, T. (1991). The revival of consciousness in cognitive science. In W. Kessen, A. Ortony, & F. Craik (Eds.), *Memories, thoughts, emotions: Essays in honor of George Mandler* (pp. 213–226). Hillsdale, NJ: Lawrence Erlbaum Associates.

Sheinkopf, S. (1970). *A comparative study of the affective judgments made by anomic aphasics and normals on a nonverbal task*. Unpublished doctoral dissertation, Boston University, Boston, MA.

Sherrington, C. S. (1933). *The brain and its mechanism*. Cambridge, England: Cambridge University Press.

Shiffrin, R. M., & Schneider, W. (1977). Controlled and automatic human information processing: II Perceptual learning, automatic attending, and a general theory. *Psychological Review, 84*, 127–190.

Simon, H. A. (1956). Rational choice and the structure of the environment. *Psychological Review, 63*, 129–138.

Skinner, B. F. (1964). Behaviorism at fifty. In T. W. Wann (Ed.), *Behaviorism and phenomenology* (pp. 79–97). Chicago: University of Chicago Press.

Smart, J. J. C. (1959). Sensations and brain processes. *Philosophical Review, 68*, 141–156.

Smith, S. M., & Vela, E. (1991). Incubated reminiscence effects. *Memory & Cognition, 19*, 168–176.

Sober, E. (1985). Panglossian functionalism and the philosophy of mind. *Synthese, 64*, 165–193.

Spence, D. P., & Holland, B. (1962). The restricting effects of awareness: A paradox and an explanation. *Journal of Abnormal and Social Psychology, 64*, 163–174.

Sperling, G. (1967). Successive approximations to a model for short-term memory. *Acta Psychologica, 27*, 285–292.

Strawson, G. (2000, 27 October 2000). Esprit de core. *The Times Literary Supplement*, 12–13.

Thagard, P. (1986). Parallel computation and the mind–body problem. *Cognitive Science, 10*, 301–318.

Thatcher, R. W., & John, E. R. (1977). *Foundations of cognitive processes.* Hillsdale, N. J.: Lawrence Erlbaum Associates.

Treisman, A. (1969). Strategies and models of selective attention. *Psychological Review, 76*, 282–299.

Treisman, A. M. (1964). Verbal cues, language and meaning in selective attention. *American Journal of Psychology, 77*, 206–218.

Treisman, A. M., & Gelade, G. (1980). A feature-integration theory of attention. *Cognitive Psychology, 12*, 97–136.

Tulving, E. (1985). Memory and consciousness. *Canadian Psychology, 26*, 1–12.

Tulving, E. (1986). What kind of a hypothesis is the distinction between episodic and semantic memory? *Journal of Experimental Psychology: Learning, Memory, and Cognition, 12*, 307–311.

Turner, T. J., & Ortony, A. (1992). Basic emotions: Can conflicting criteria converge? *Psychological Rewview, 99*, 566–571.

Tversky, A. (1972). Elimination by aspects: A theory of choice. *Psychological Review, 79*, 281–299.

Van Gulick, R. (1980). Functionalism, information and content. *Nature and System, 2*, 139–162.

Van Gulick, R. (1988). Consciousness, intrinsic intentionality, and self-understanding machines. In A. M. E. Bisiach (Ed.), *Consciousness in contemporary science* (pp. 78–100). Oxford, England: Clarendon Press/Oxford University Press.

Vygotsky, L. S. (1962). *Thought and language.* Cambridge, Mass.: M. I. T. Press.

Warrington, E. K. (1975). The selective impairment of semantic memory. *Quarterly Journal of Experimental Psychology, 27*, 635–657.

Watts, A. W. (1957). *The way of Zen.* New York: Pantheon Books.

Weinberg, S. (1995). Reductionism redux. *The New York Review of Books, 62 (No. 15)*, 39–42.

Weiskrantz, L. (1985). On issues and theories of the human amnesic syndrome. In N. M. Weinberger, J. L. McGaugh, & G. Lynch (Eds.), *Memory systems of the brain: Animal and human cognitive processes* (pp. 380–415). New York: Guilford Press.

Weiskrantz, L. (1986). *Blindsight: A case study and implications.* Oxford: Clarendon Press.

West, L. J., & Farber, I. E. (1960). The role of pain in emotional development. In L. J. West & M. Greenblatt (Eds.), *Explorations in the physiology of emotions* (pp. 119–126). Washington, D.C.: American Psychiatric Association.

Woodward, A. E., Bjork, R. A., & Jongeward, R. H. J. (1973). Recall and recognition as a function of primary rehearsal. *Journal of Verbal Learning an Verbal Behavior, 12,* 608–617.

Yaniv, I., & Meyer, D. E. (1987). Activation and metacognition of inaccessible stored information: Potential bases for incubation effects in problem solving. *Journal of Experimental Psychology: Learning, Memory, and Cognition, 13,* 187–205.

Zborowski, M. (1969). *People in pain.* San Francisco: Jossey-Bass.

Books, chapters, and papers used in part in preparation of this book

Mandler, G. (1975). Consciousness: Respectable, useful, and probably necessary. In R. Solso (Ed.), *Information processing and cognition: The Loyola symposium.* Hillsdale, New Jersey: Lawrence Erlbaum Associates, Inc. Also Technical Report No. 41, Center for Human Information Processing, UCSD, March, 1974.

Mandler, G. (1984). The construction and limitation of consciousness. In V. Sarris and A. Parducci (Eds.) *Perspectives in psychological experimentation: Toward the year 2000.* Hillside, N.J.: Lawrence Erlbaum Associates. German translation: Aufbau und Grenzen des Bewusstseins. In V. Sarris and A. Parducci (Eds.) *Die Zukunft der experimentellen Psychologie.* Weinheim und Basel: Beltz, 1986.

Mandler, G.(1984). *Mind and body: Psychology of emotion and stress.* New York: Norton. Science Book Club selection, 1985. Japanese edition: Seishin Shobo Publishers, 1987.

Mandler, G. (1985). *Cognitive psychology: An essay in cognitive science.* Hillsdale, N.J.: Lawrence Erlbaum Associates. Japanese edition: Kinokuniya Publishers, 1991. Ch. 3 (Consciousness) reprinted in J. Pickering and M. Skinner (Eds.) *From sentence to symbols: Readings on consciousness.* Hemel Hempstead: Harvester-Wheatsheaf, 1990. Pp. 156–165.

Mandler, G., and Nakamura, Y. (1987). Aspects of consciousness. *Personality and Social Psychology Bulletin,* pp. 299–313.

Mandler, G. (1987). Explorations in consciousness. William James Award address, Division of General Psychology, American Psychological Association meetings, August.

Mandler, G. (1988). Problems and directions in the study of consciousness. In M. Horowitz (Ed.) *Psychodynamics and cognition.* Chicago: Univ. of Chicago Press. Translation in G. Hatano et al. (Eds.) Cognitive Science Handbook. Tokyo: Kyoritsu Shuppan, 1992.

Mandler, G. (1989). Memory: Conscious and unconscious. In P.R. Solomon, G.R. Goethals, C.M. Kelley, and B.R. Stephens (Eds.) *Memory: Interdisplinary approaches.* New York: Springer Verlag.

Mandler, G. (1989). Activation, elaboration, and consciousness. In A.F. Bennett & K.M. McConkey (Eds.) *Cognition in individual and social contexts.* Amsterdam: Elsevier

Mandler, G. (1992). Toward a theory of consciousness. In H.-G. Geissler, S.W. Link & J.T. Townsend (Eds.) *Cognition, information processing, and psychophysics: Basic issues.* Hillsdale, N.J.: Lawrence Erlbaum Associates.

Mandler, G. (1993). Thought, memory, and learning: Effects of emotional stress. In L. Goldberger and S. Breznitz (Eds.), *Handbook of stress: Theoretical and clinical aspects.* (2nd edition). New York: Free Press/Macmillan. Incorporates: Mandler, G. (1979).

Thought processes, consciousness, and stress. In V. Hamilton and D.A. Warburton (Eds.) *Human stress and cognition: An information processing approach.* London: John Wiley & Sons, Ltd.

Mandler, G. (1994). Hypermnesia,incubation, and mind-popping: On remembering without really trying. In C. Umiltà & M. Moscovitch (Eds.), *Attention and Performance XV: Conscious and nonconsciousinformation processing.* Cambridge, Mass.: MIT Press

Mandler, G. (1997). Consciousness redux. In J.D. Cohen and J.W. Schooler (Eds.) *Scientific approaches to consciousness: The Twentyfifth Annual Carnegie Symposium on Cognition.* Hillsdale, NJ: Lawrence Erlbaum Associates.

Mandler, G. (1997). What is it that consciousness lets us do that we could not do otherwise? In H. Mandl (Ed.) *Bericht über den 40. Kongreß der Deutschen Gesellschaft für Psychologie in München 1996.* Hogrefe — Verlag für Psychologie, Göttingen.

Mandler, G. (1997). *Human nature explored.* New York: Oxford University Press

Mandler, G. (1998). Consciousness and mind as philosophical problems and as psychological issues. In J. Hochberg (Ed.) *Perception & Cognition at Century's End.* San Diego: Academic Press.

Index of Names

Index of Subjects